# About This Book

## Why is this topic important?

Participants will not feel the impact of training activities unless they are highly experiential. Experiential activities utilize games, simulations, role play, visualization, and many other methods. These methods allow participants to engage both their minds and their emotions. The result is that the activities are "unforgettable." Not only do participants remember the activity for a long time but their learning is deepened and their desire to make changes is strengthened. Effective experiential activities often have an element of surprise and drama. This book contains seventy-five "unforgettable" training activities, all designed by experiential guru Mel Silberman, culled from his thirty-five-year career as a trainer and developer.

## What can you achieve with this book?

This book is a resource a trainer can use again and again to find experiential activities that fit a wide variety of training topics. Both new and experienced trainers will benefit from this collection. With step-by-step instructions, along with alternative options, a trainer's repertoire of engaging activities will increase. Moreover, this book contains suggestions about the most important ways to design and facilitate experiential learning.

## How is this book organized?

This book begins with a useful introduction to the design and facilitation of experiential activities. Following this are seventy-five experiential activities covering fifteen training topics, such as Leadership, Train the Trainer, Team Building, Creativity and Problem Solving, Conflict and Negotiation, Sales and Customer Service, and Diversity.

# About Pfeiffer

Pfeiffer serves the professional development and hands-on resource needs of training and human resource practitioners and gives them products to do their jobs better. We deliver proven ideas and solutions from experts in HR development and HR management, and we offer effective and customizable tools to improve workplace performance. From novice to seasoned professional, Pfeiffer is the source you can trust to make yourself and your organization more successful.

**Essential Knowledge** Pfeiffer produces insightful, practical, and comprehensive materials on topics that matter the most to training and HR professionals. Our Essential Knowledge resources translate the expertise of seasoned professionals into practical, how-to guidance on critical workplace issues and problems. These resources are supported by case studies, worksheets, and job aids and are frequently supplemented with CD-ROMs, websites, and other means of making the content easier to read, understand, and use.

**Essential Tools** Pfeiffer's Essential Tools resources save time and expense by offering proven, ready-to-use materials—including exercises, activities, games, instruments, and assessments—for use during a training or team-learning event. These resources are frequently offered in looseleaf or CD-ROM format to facilitate copying and customization of the material.

Pfeiffer also recognizes the remarkable power of new technologies in expanding the reach and effectiveness of training. While e-hype has often created whizbang solutions in search of a problem, we are dedicated to bringing convenience and enhancements to proven training solutions. All our e-tools comply with rigorous functionality standards. The most appropriate technology wrapped around essential content yields the perfect solution for today's on-the-go trainers and human resource professionals.

**Pfeiffer**
www.pfeiffer.com

*Essential resources for training and HR professionals*

# Unforgettable

## Experiential
## Activities

### An Active Training™ Resource

**Mel Silberman**

**Pfeiffer**

A Wiley Imprint

www.pfeiffer.com

An Imprint of Wiley
989 Market Street, San Francisco, CA 94103-1741
www.pfeiffer.com

For additional copies/bulk purchases of this book in the U.S. please contact 800-274-4434.

Pfeiffer books and products are available through most bookstores. To contact Pfeiffer directly call our Customer Care Department within the U.S. at 800-274-4434, outside the U.S. at 317-572-3985, fax 317-572-4002, or visit www.pfeiffer.com.

Pfeiffer also publishes its books in a variety of electronic formats. Some content that appears in print may not be available in electronic books.

**Library of Congress Cataloging-in-Publication Data**
Silberman, Melvin L.
      Unforgettable experiential activities/Mel Silberman.
          p.   cm.
      ISBN 978-0-470-53714-5 (pbk.)
      1. Employees—Training of.   2. Effective teaching.   I. Title.
      HF5549.5.T7S55545 2010
      658.3'124—dc22
                                                                    2010000286

Acquiring Editor: Holly Allen                    Director of Development: Kathleen Dolan Davies

Production Editor: Dawn Kilgore                   Editor: Rebecca Taff

Editorial Assistant: Lindsay Morton              Manufacturing Supervisor: Becky Morgan

Printed in the United States of America

Printing  10 9 8 7 6 5 4 3 2 1

# CONTENTS

Preface................................................................................ix

Acknowledgments ...........................................................xiii

Foreword..........................................................................xv

Introduction.......................................................................1

**Chapter One: Getting Acquainted**                              **11**

   1. Alphabetical Circle: A Fun Way to Learn Names and a Lot More .........12

   2. Group Résumé: Who We Are Collectively ................................14

   3. Things We Have in Common: Getting to Know You ...................16

   4. Predictions: Making Guesses About Co-Participants...................18

   5. Introductory Go-Arounds: Brief Self-Disclosures ....................20

   6. What's in a Name? My Story ...............................................22

**Chapter Two: Communication**                                  **25**

   7. Communication Tokens: An Awareness Exercise....................26

   8. Direct Communication: You Write the Scripts........................28

   9. Explaining Something Complicated: Avoiding Information Dumps......30

  10. Obtaining Participation: Using Different Formats....................34

**Chapter Three: Assertive Behavior**                           **41**

  11. Concerns About Confronting Employees: Overcoming the Anxiety .....42

  12. Assertive Starters: Ways to Begin an Assertive Message...........46

  13. Non-Verbal Persuasion: Assessing Its Impact .......................50

14. Refusing Unwanted Requests: Practicing Saying No ....................52

15. Stating Complaints and Requesting Change: Skill Practice ....................56

**Chapter Four: Influencing Others**                                         **59**

16. Alligator River: Looking at People with Different Glasses ....................60

17. Question First: The Best Way to Overcome Resistance ....................65

18. Influencing Others: Four Role-Play Scenarios ....................68

19. Getting Your Foot in the Door: Avoiding Rejection ....................72

**Chapter Five: Conflict and Negotiation**                                   **75**

20. Views of Conflict: A Word Association Game ....................76

21. What You Bring to Conflict Situations: Experiencing Different Styles ...79

22. The Ten-Thousand-Dollar Challenge: Working Through a Conflict ....................85

23. Role Reversal: Arguing the Flip Side ....................89

24. Rating Methods to Deal with Conflict: Yours and Theirs ....................92

25. Breaking a Stalemate: Steps to Move Forward ....................95

**Chapter Six: Creativity and Problem Solving**                              **99**

26. Getting Ready for Brainstorming: Creative Warm-Ups ....................100

27. Part Changing: Demonstrating a Technique to Increase Creativity ....................105

28. Brainwriting: An Alternative to Generating Ideas Verbally ....................108

29. Inspired Cut-Outs: Freeing the Mind ....................110

30. Wearing Someone Else's Shoes: Taking a Different Perspective ....................113

31. Making Decisions After Brainstorming: Narrowing the Options ....................116

**Chapter Seven: Diversity**                                                 **119**

32. Being in the Minority: Simulating an Everyday Reality ....................120

33. I've Been Curious: Questions I Have Been Afraid to Ask ....................124

34. Setting the Record Straight: Things About Me and Others Like Me ....127

35. Unlocking Memories: Self-Disclosures in a Diverse Group ....................130

**Chapter Eight: Facilitating Teams** **133**

36. Multi-Voting: A Constructive Way to Make Decisions............................134

37. Rotating Facilitators: Practicing Effective Facilitation .........................137

38. Card Exchange: A Unique Way to Stimulate Discussion........................142

39. The Problem with Majority Voting: A Double Whammy......................145

40. Changing the Rules: Altering Group Process .........................................148

41. Removing Egos: A Tool for Team Facilitators........................................151

**Chapter Nine: Exchanging Feedback** **155**

42. Animal Metaphors: An Exercise in Obtaining Honest Feedback..........156

43. Giving Effective Feedback: Wheaties Over Donuts ..............................163

44. Judging the Impact of Words: Applications to Giving Feedback..........168

45. When Asking for or Giving Feedback Is Challenging: Your Advice ......173

**Chapter Ten: Leadership** **177**

46. The Window Shade: Depicting Different Approaches to
Decision Making .....................................................................................178

47. Mirroring: Experiencing the Joys and Tribulations
of Being a Leader ....................................................................................181

48. Going Outside Comfort Zones: Brief Exercises in Change ..................185

49. Changes You Would Make: Dreaming Beyond the Status Quo ............190

**Chapter Eleven: Teaching and Coaching Employees** **195**

50. Making Butterflies: It's Not What You Say That Counts ......................196

51. Brain-Friendly Teaching: Using Four Key Principles ...........................202

52. Building Skills Through Role Plays: You Have Options........................208

53. The Components of Effective Coaching: Observing the Process..........218

54. Show But Not Tell: Upping the Stakes .................................................218

**Chapter Twelve: Understanding Others** **221**

55. Avoiding Labels: Interpreting Behavior Objectively .............................222

56. Be Curious, Not Furious: Five Ways to Understand Others...................227

57. Comparing Yourself to Others: Looking for
    Differences and Similarities........................................................231

58. The Three C's: What Makes People Difficult.............................234


**Chapter Thirteen: Sales and Customer Service**                         **239**

59. A Convincing Sales Presentation: Warm-up Practice ...........240

60. Dissatisfied Customers: How to Win Them Over .................243

61. To Consult or Not Consult: Assessing Your Selling Style .......248

62. Your Company's Sales Philosophy: How Do You Treat Customers?......251


**Chapter Fourteen: Team Building**                                      **255**

63. The Stages of Team Development: A Card Sorting Activity...................256

64. Television Commercial: An Unusual Team-Building Activity ...............262

65. Creative House Building: An Exercise in Teamwork............................264

66. Fishbowl Meeting: Observing Group Process.................................266

67. Making Paper Cups: Simulating a Learning Organization...................269

68. Are You a Team Player? Things Team Players Do.............................274

69. Paper Airplanes: The Power of Collaboration .............................278


**Chapter Fifteen: Train the Trainer**                                   **281**

70. Active Vacations: Topics Versus Objectives.................................282

71. Design Challenges: Planning How to Achieve Training Objectives......286

72. Energizers: Ways to Wake Up or Relax a Training Group ...............289

73. Has This Ever Happened to You? Making Team Learning Work..........292

74. Training Styles: Three Continua.............................................296

75. You Have Many Options: Increasing Your Training Repertoire...........298


**About the Author** ....................................................................**301**

# PREFACE

This collection of experiential activities is almost entirely original. The activities are my creations drawn from my nearly forty-year training career. Some will sound familiar because activity designers share so much and learn so much from one another. For example, they may use a common experience, such as making paper airplanes. Or they make similar points such as, "collaboration is better than competition." However, you will find that the activities that follow contain subtle or unique differences from the many creative efforts of my other colleagues.

Of course, nothing can be entirely original. Minds think alike. But even well-known activities can be contextualized to make different points. When I use a frequently traveled idea, such as changing how you interlace your fingers, you will discover how I use the idea in a way that is not common.

Some of the activities are based on material from my over twenty publications on active training. The one book you may be familiar with—*101 Ways to Make Training Active*—may appear to be a similar collection. The difference here is that *Unforgettable Experiential Activities* is not a collection of training strategies for virtually any topic or situation. Instead, this collection contains only activity designs applied to specific topics. None of the topics, however, is mutually exclusive. What I classify as an activity on "leadership" can be useful to another category, such as "facilitating teams." Hopefully, the sorting is helpful to you in navigating through this collection to find what you need.

The topic areas are

- Getting Acquainted
- Communication
- Assertive Behavior

- Influencing Others
- Conflict and Negotiation
- Creativity and Problem Solving
- Diversity
- Facilitating Teams
- Exchanging Feedback
- Leadership
- Teaching and Coaching Employees
- Understanding Others
- Sales and Customer Service
- Team Building
- Train the Trainer

The activities tend to focus on one or two different goals within each area:

- Awareness (how it feels to confront another person) and/or
- Skill practice (stating complaints without putting others down).

The book begins with an introduction to experiential activities. You will learn some of their unique features and benefits as well as tips to facilitate them effectively.

Following the introduction are seventy-five experiential activities, sorted into the fifteen areas previously listed. Each activity begins with introductory remarks that provide a general overview. Often, I will take the liberty of mentioning how I have used the activity in my training career and other personal comments about my attraction to the activity in question. Following these remarks is a brief statement of the activity's objectives. I then give you information about the optimal group size for the activity, the time required, and materials needed. (You should be able to make adjustments to the information provided if necessary or desired.) Each activity write-up ends with a section called "other options." Here you will be given other ideas to modify or completely change the activity to suit your needs.

So explore and discover unforgettable experiential activities you can use to advance your training prowess.

MEL SILBERMAN
Princeton, N.J.
December 2009

# ACKNOWLEDGMENTS

Since this collection represents my entire career as a designer of experiential activities, there are countless individuals from whom I have learned how to approach this task. You are all the object of my sincerest appreciation.

The first person to model the idea of making training unforgettable and inspire me to try it out myself is Rod Napier. Rod's creative, memorable, and challenging ideas I witnessed more than thirty-five years ago. It showed me a whole other way to engage adults . . . without lecturing and fear that they would resist immediate involvement. At times, I thought he was taking dangerous risks, but I gradually learned that it was that risk taking that enables one to forge ahead as an expert facilitator of experiential learning. Thank you, Rod.

Other notable people have served as role models. Here are just a few them: Thiagi, Sharon Bowman, Garry Shirts, Bernie DeKoven, Sandra Fowler, Kevin Eikenberry, Bob Pike, and Jean Barbazette.

Freda Hansburg, Karen Lawson, and Kim Stott, all former students of mine, have been wonderful partners in my experimentation with experiential learning.

I am especially grateful to all the creative people I have known and observed at conferences of the North American Association for Gaming and Simulation.

As ever, I am appreciative of the good people at Pfeiffer, who are always behind my writing. I wish to single out Susan Rachmeler and Holly Allen. In the recent past, Martin Delahoussaye has been one of my strongest boosters.

As ever, I have deep pockets of supporters from my closest personal friends. My family has been there and loved me unconditionally . . . my children Shmuel, Lisa, and Gabe, my son-in-law and daughter-in-law Daniel and Sara, and my precious grandchildren, Noam, Jonah, Yaakov, Adira, Meir, and Chana. The greatest source of support and love comes from my wife of forty-six years, Shoshana. She is a special woman with wisdom and untiring devotion. Good luck has followed me all my life, and she is central to this fortune.

# FOREWORD

## By Jane Bozarth

I was a contributor to *Training Magazine's* "In Print" book review column from its inception in 2000 until the magazine's demise in 2010. Various editors had various ways of asking the review team to rate the books, from numbers-of-stars to something resembling a temperature gauge. In 2005, when I reviewed the newly-released second edition of Mel Silberman's *101 Ways to Make Training Active,* the rating system in place was a scale of Buy—Borrow—Don't Bother. For Mel Silberman's work I made up a new category: Buy Now.

My own personal curse as a training practitioner—spent entirely in government practice—is the somewhat mixed-blessing talent for being good at designing and delivering policy and compliance training. Because of this, I was called on to do it many, many times, and in most of those instances something from Mel Silberman helped me overcome the tedium of the content. His ideas were practical, meaningful, and fun, and eminently applicable, right then, that day. His suggestions for making training active were often also a trainer's dream, requiring little setup and few props, and as often as not, Mel offered ideas for applying an activity to assorted topics. This final book, *Unforgettable Experiential Activities,* is an exception to that last, with Mel offering ideas suited to specific types of subject matter or training topic.

Mel was prolific, from the first edition of *101 Ways* in 1995 to this last work. Readers knew he turned out one and often more titles a year; few knew that he struggled with the insidious monster that is cancer for most of that time. While he is justifiably famous for his "active training" mantra, many readers may also not know: that Mel was a popular, beloved professor at

Temple; that his first book offered tips on parenting; and that his next-to-last work, *Active Jewish Training,* was a work of love written with his wife of forty-six years, Shoshana.

The back cover copy for one of Mel's books offers an endorsement from an author/trainer who describes his work as "sparkling." With Mel's passing, the training world sparkles a little less brightly.

# INTRODUCTION

After a while, participants will usually forget a great presentation, but rarely do they forget a great activity.

**What makes a training activity *unforgettable*?**

What participants remember is that they had an EXPERIENCE that they will always remember, not just the next day but days and perhaps years later.

In his book *The Tipping Point,* Malcolm Gladwell (2000) uses the term "stickiness" to identify why some ideas, practices, and products capture the public's imagination. Effective experiential activities are "sticky." When they are done well, they adhere to you. This happens for several reasons:

- Experiential activities are concrete. They are based on specific events, not on intellectual abstractions.

- Experiential activities feature participatory methods, such as games, role play, unique discussion formats, visualization, and more.

- Experiential activities are dramatic. They arouse participants' emotions. They stir feelings of joy, wonder, and sometimes discomfort.

- Experiential activities often surprise, even jolt participants. The experience is not what participants expected.

You can try your own hand at creating experiential activities. Here are some tips:

1. Many experiential activities can be found not only in this collection but in other publications. Don't limit yourself to the published version of an experiential activity. Change the materials, the directions, and the ultimate learning points to create the surprise you want. Or add new elements.

2. Try out the activity for the first time in a setting where the outcome does not have to be perfect. Watch how the activity unfolds. Note changes to make for the next time you use the activity so that it moves smoothly and creates the effect you are seeking.

3. Pay careful attention to how participants behave during the exercise. They may do something that you didn't count on, and this event may lead to a new learning point you hadn't anticipated.

4. Many experiential activities are metaphorical. The actual activity going on is analogous to or symbolic of something important in real life. Make sure, however, that the connection between the activity and real life is not far-fetched. If it is, participants will not buy in. Alter the activity to make the comparison stronger.

5. Don't seek to make only one point when more than one flows from the activity you have chosen. Expand the richness of the activity.

The best experiential activities are not simply events. The richest part of the activity is the conversation that follows. Often referred to as the *debriefing*, it allows the participants to probe what happened during the activity, the implications and learnings that flow from the activity, and action steps to consider so that the activity leads not only to learner involvement but to potential change.

I would recommend using the *What? So What? Now What?* debriefing model. (Some of the activity designs will deliberately use this format.) The concept behind it is to separate the debriefing into three sections. Here's how you do it:

1. Ask participants to share what happened to them during the experience:
   - What did they do?
   - What did they observe? Think about?
   - What feelings did they have during the experience?

2. Next ask participants to ask themselves "so what?"
   - What benefits did they get from the experience?
   - What did they learn? Relearn?

- What are the implications of the activity?
- How does the experience (if it is a simulation or role play) relate to the real world?

3. Finally, ask participants to consider "now what?"

- How do they want to do things differently in the future?
- How can they extend the learning?
- What steps can they take to apply what they learned?

Here is an example of the model in action:

In a session on conflict resolution, participants are asked to form pairs. The trainer tells them that, at the sound of the whistle, they are to thumb wrestle their partners for two minutes. At the end of the time period, the trainer blows the whistle again to stop the action. The trainer processes the activity by asking the following questions:

**What?**

- How did you behave during the thumb wrestling?
- What feelings did you have as you were thumb wrestling?

**So What?**

- What did you learn about your own approach to conflict?
- How do you deal with conflict in real life?

**Now What?**

- How do you want to deal with conflict on the job or in your personal life in the future?

Finally, as you conduct experiential activities, try to avoid these common mistakes:

1. *Motivation*: Participants aren't invited to buy into the activity or sold on the benefits of joining in. Participants don't know what to expect during the exercise.

2. *Direction:* Instructions are lengthy and unclear. Participants cannot visualize what the trainer expects from them.

3. *Group process:* When used, subgroups are not composed effectively. Group formats are not changed to fit the requirements of each activity. Subgroups are left idle.

4. *Energy:* Activities move too slowly. Participants are sedentary. Activities are long or demanding when they need to be short or relaxed. Participants do not find the activity challenging.

5. *Debriefing:* Participants are confused and/or overwhelmed by the questions put to them. The trainer's questions don't promote the goals of the activity. The trainer shares her or his opinions before hearing the participants' views.

Instead, here are some suggestions.

# Motivating Participation

Your participants need to be tempted before they will feel motivated to join in and take the exercise seriously. Getting participants to buy into an activity is essential to the success of your planned exercise, especially if it involves risk or effort. Here are some ways to motivate participation:

1. *Explain your objectives.* Participants like to know what is going to happen and why. Don't assume that they know your objectives. Make sure they do.

2. *Sell the benefits.* Tell participants what's in it for them. Explain what benefits they will derive back on the job as a result of the activity.

3. *Convey enthusiasm.* If you sound motivated about seeing them engaged in an activity, participants will internalize some of your enthusiasm.

4. *Connect the activity to previous activities.* Explaining the relationship between activities helps participants to see the common thread in your program.

5. *Share personal feelings with participants.* Explain why you have found the activity (or one like it) valuable to you.

6. *Express confidence in participants.* Tell participants that you think they'll do a good job with the activity or that they are now ready to tackle a new challenge.

# Directing Participants' Activities

Incomplete or unclear instructions can spell disaster for an experiential activity. If you do not take the time to explain exactly how the exercise should be completed, participants may spend more time asking questions about what they were supposed to be doing than actually taking part in the activity. Although you need to be careful not to sound like a schoolteacher, don't be afraid of oversimplifying; there is always someone who needs clarification and repetition. Here are four tips for making sure that the group understands your directions:

1. *Speak slowly.* Listening to instructions to a complex activity is harder than listening to a lecture. Slow down so that participants can follow you.

2. *Use visual backup.* If appropriate, write directions on a handout or flip chart and allow participants to refer to this visual information as you orally explain it.

3. *Define important terms.* Don't take for granted that every participant will understand the key words in your instructions the same way you do. Explain important directions in more than one way.

4. *Demonstrate the activity.* Sometimes it is important for participants to have a mental picture of what they are to do. Provide a brief sample of what the activity will look like. Use yourself and/or a few participants to illustrate the instructions.

# Managing the Group Process

Most experiential activities involve subgrouping. Small groups give participants an opportunity to discuss ideas and ask questions in greater detail than is possible in a large-group format. Group movement also accommodates the diverse personal learning styles of your participants, many of whom may feel more comfortable speaking in a small group than they do when all of the participants are together.

Managing this process of forming and monitoring subgroups is difficult because you cannot completely control how participants will behave in smaller units. Also, some participants may not be as comfortable, at least initially, in subgroups as they are when the full group is together. Here are some suggestions to maximize peer interaction and productive work.

1. *Form groups in a variety of ways.* In order to separate acquaintances or randomize group composition, assign numbers to participants after they have seated themselves and then form groups corresponding to those numbers. Or allow participants to choose their own partners when you want to encourage friends to work together. When you want to achieve a certain composition, form groups according to specific criteria (for example, by gender or department).

   Count the number of participants as soon as you believe that you have full attendance. Then determine how large your subgroups will be by finding a number that easily divides into your total number of participants. Twelve is the easiest number of participants to work with; a group of this size can be divided into subgroups of two, three, or four members without your having to join the last group to make it even.

2. *Mix teams and seat partners.* Mixing up groupings offers the participants the chance to get a broad range of opinions and adds interesting variety to their discussions. Keep teams and seat partners together for long periods only when you need continuity. Set place cards in new locations in the training room to change seating patterns and create new seat partners.

3. *Vary the number of people in any activity based on that exercise's specific requirements.* The smaller the group, the more opportunities for each participant to contribute. Work with the number of participants in your course to create groups whose sizes fit your design's requirements. If possible, try to keep work groups to six people or fewer to maximize individual participation. Include yourself if subgroup adjustments have to be made.

4. *Divide participants into teams before giving further directions.* Ask participants to move to their new locations first, and then describe the particulars of how to conduct the exercise. Many trainers have to repeat directions for an activity because the participants forget them by the time subgroups are formed.

5. *Ask groups of five or more to elect a facilitator or timekeeper.* Larger groups can be difficult to keep on track and on time. A facilitator for each group relieves you of that burden.

6. *Give groups instructions separately in a multipart activity.* Subgroups may finish their assignments at different times. Instead of waiting for all groups to finish one section of a multipart activity, quietly give the next set of directions to each subgroup when it is ready to move on.

7. *Keep people busy.* If one subgroup finishes all its work well in advance of the other groups, sit down with the group to review what group members have done. If it is clear that more is needed, ask them to do it in the time remaining.

8. *Inform the subgroups how much time they have.* State the time allotted for the entire activity and then announce periodically how much time remains. Visit subgroups to see how much they have accomplished. When you are about to stop a group activity, give the participants a warning.

Say, "You'll have ten minutes to do this activity. Make sure each person gets a two-minute turn. . . . You should be about halfway around the group by now. . . . There are two minutes left. . . . Please wrap up your discussions now so that we can get back together as a full group."

A trainer who quietly and smoothly manages group process is rarely noticed; the chaotic atmosphere of the training course will give away one who does so clumsily. For example, an activity that calls for the participants to work together in pairs would be awkwardly set up by the instructions, "Pair up with the person seated next to you" (Did you mean the person on the left or the right?). Such pairing can be facilitated gracefully by pointing out two participants at a time and saying, "You two are a pair, and you two, and you two. . . ." It is simple moves like these that give the participants a clear indication of what to do.

# *Keeping Participants Involved*

Your job is not over once the participants have been organized into groups and begin working on an experiential activity. You may find yourself redesigning an activity on the spot if it seems to be too long, short, simple, or complex for a particular situation. Altering a training design to fit the time of day and the mood of your participants helps to keep the energy level of your training group up and active. Redesigning also adds interest and fun. Go with what is happening in the room if it meets your training goals. If an activity or exercise yields an unexpected surprise or draws an unusual response from your participants, make a training moment happen by weaving that surprise response into what you are trying to achieve educationally. The ability to be flexible within the design of a planned activity adds energy to the exercise for both you and your participants. Here are some other guidelines for sustaining group energy:

1. *Keep the activity moving.* Don't slow things down by speaking very slowly, endlessly recording participants' contributions on flip charts, or letting a discussion drag on too long. Usually, more energy is generated when participants have to complete an activity within a specific time. Keep time frames short and move things along at a brisk pace.

2. *Challenge the participants.* There is more energy when activities create a moderate level of tension. If tasks are a snap, participants will become lethargic. Emphasize the importance of a challenging activity and encourage participants to really think about their answers or try out new behaviors.

3. *Reinforce participants for their involvement in the activity.* Show interest in the participants as they engage in the activity. Don't stand off or busy yourself with other things. Show that you are really interested in how they are doing and praise success.

4. *Build physical movement into the activity.* Have participants move their chairs, stand up, or use their entire bodies during the activity as a way to wake them up.

5. *Let your enthusiasm show.* Genuine feelings of excitement and enjoyment about an activity will inspire like emotions in the participants. Your high energy level can lift up the energy level of the entire group.

Behaviors that energize participants can be easily woven into your facilitation style. Once your experiential training designs are joined with these behaviors, you'll become both effective and believable as you reinforce participant involvement. Using these behaviors in the classroom will help you to accomplish your educational objectives while maintaining high levels of energy and interest in your planned activities.

# *Debriefing the Activity*

As I have already emphasized, when an activity has concluded, it's quite important for participants to process it—that is, to discuss any feelings that the activity elicited and to share their final reflections and insights. Debriefing questions help to complete the learning cycle by collating information gathered by the participants during the activity and applying that information within the context of the subject of the training program. Here are some tips to help you facilitate the debriefing portion of an activity.

1. *Ask relevant questions.* Often, trainers think they are debriefing activities merely by asking participants questions such as "Did you like the activity?" or "Was it worthwhile?" Following are some examples of debriefing questions that encourage participants to go beyond simple answers and invite responses related to training goals. Be careful, however, not to ask too many debriefing questions at once. Usually one to three questions are all a group can handle at a time.

   ■ "What were your reactions to the activity?"

   ■ "What did you learn?"

   ■ "What can you take away from the activity?"

2. *Carefully structure the first debriefing experiences.* A high percentage of activities invite debriefing in an active training program. Knowing this, it makes sense to train your participants to process activities in the early phases of the program. The first time you process an activity with a group, ask only one or two simple questions and keep the discussion time brief. It is probably a good idea to direct the debriefing as well. For example, you might present a question and then go around the group,

obtaining a short response from each person. Later on, less direction will be necessary.

One way to structure the debriefing of an activity is to use incomplete sentence stems. Say, "One thing I thought was worthwhile about this activity was. . . ."

3. *Observe how participants react during the debriefing.* The most valuable and productive debriefing occurs when all participants feel comfortable expressing themselves. If participants begin to give responses that are personally critical of other members of the group, step in by modeling behaviorally specific information and deal with any personal confrontation in a positive manner. Through your own behavior, you can help the group to establish an open forum that promotes the expression of personal views without personal criticisms.

4. *Assist a subgroup that is having trouble debriefing an activity.* If you have asked subgroups to process an activity and one group finishes well before the time you have allotted expires, it's likely that they have experienced difficulty debriefing and have wrapped up their reactions too quickly, without probing below the surface. You can help them take a more in-depth look at the implications of an activity by asking them to share with you what they have discussed and then extending the discussion by probing further.

5. *Keep your own reactions to yourself until after you've heard from the participants.* Let the participants know that you respect them for their opinions. The debriefing time is primarily their opportunity to discover what can be learned from the activity. Your insights may be welcomed, but save them for the end.

# **Reference**

Gladwell, M. (2000). *The tipping point.* Boston, MA: Little Brown and Co.

# 1 GETTING ACQUAINTED

**Alphabetical Circle: A Fun Way to Learn Names and a Lot More**

## Introductory Remarks

This activity gives a unique twist to traditional introductions. Participants are asked to form a circle and then rearrange themselves in alphabetical order by first names. One challenge is that they must remove any name badges and use only sign language. The second is that they are not told in which direction the alphabetical order goes—clockwise or counterclockwise. It's a fun activity with many interesting debriefing possibilities.

## Objectives

- To experience a novel way for people to get to know each others' names.
- To begin training with a challenging task.

**Group Size:** eight to eighteen participants

**Time Required:** 10 minutes

**Materials:** none

## Activity Flow

1. Ask participants to form a circle. Ask them to remove any name badges. Quickly, have each participant say the first name he or she wants to use during the training, starting with the person to your right or left. (Include yourself in the introductions.)

2. Next, ask participants to rearrange themselves alphabetically without talking. Any other nonverbal strategies are allowed. If asked for the direction of the circle (clockwise or counterclockwise), tell the group they can choose (without using words).

3. As the newly arranged circle emerges, observe what is happening (don't play an active role). Are some people lining up clockwise while others are counterclockwise? Which participants are taking leadership roles? Which participants are passive?

4. When the group seems to be finished, have each person say his or her name in alphabetical order. If they discover that the group has used two ways of lining up or if a person is out of place, let participants rearrange themselves.

5. Go around the group, asking each person to say his or her name and one unusual fact about him- or herself.

6. Debrief the activity with the following questions:

   ▪ How difficult was it to communicate your first initial without talking?

   ▪ (If appropriate) When did you realize that the circle was formed in two different ways?

   ▪ What did you do to assist the group to be successful?

   ▪ Was there a conflict among "leaders"?

# Other Options

1. Have each participant give nonverbal signals conveying his or her first name. Let other participants take guesses until correct.

2. As participants enter the room, have them sign in alphabetically. They can erase another person's name and reenter it somewhere else.

## 2 Group Résumé: Who We Are Collectively

**Introductory Remarks**

Résumés typically describe an individual's accomplishments. A group résumé is a fun way to help participants become acquainted or do some team building with a training group whose members already know one another. This activity can be especially effective if the résumé is geared to the subject matter of the training.

## Objectives

- To learn information about the participants in a group.
- To build connections among participants.

**Group Size:** any

**Time Required:** 10 minutes per group to prepare and another 5 minutes per group to present

## Materials

- Newsprint and markers

## Activity Flow

1. Divide participants into subgroups of three to six members.
2. Tell the group members that they represent an incredible array of talents and experiences!

3. Suggest that one way to identify and brag about the group's resources is to compose a group résumé. (You may want to suggest a job or contract the group could be bidding for.)

4. Give the subgroups newsprint and markers to use in creating their résumés. The résumés should include any information that promotes the subgroup as a whole. The groups may choose to include any of the following information:

- Educational background

- Knowledge about the course content

- Total years of professional experience

- Positions held

- Professional skills

- Major accomplishments

- Publications

- Hobbies, talents, travel, family

5. Invite each subgroup to present its résumé. Then celebrate the total resources contained within the entire group.

# Other Options

1. To expedite the activity, give out a prepared résumé outline that specifies the information to be gathered.

2. Instead of having participants compile a résumé, ask them to interview one another about categories that you provide.

**Things We Have in Common:
Getting to Know You**

---
## Introductory Remarks

This icebreaker is a version of the well-known game *To
Tell the Truth*. I have given it a few new twists. It works as an
instant method to build cohesion. It is particularly suited
for training programs that encourage self-disclosure.
---

## *Objectives*

- To discover commonalities with other participants.

- To quickly introduce games into a training program.

**Group Size:** up to twenty

**Time Required:** 20 to 30 minutes (depending on the number of participants)

**Materials:** none

## *Activity Flow*

1. Pair off participants. If there is a participant who does not have a partner,
   become the partner for that participant.

2. Tell each pair to find as many facts about themselves *held in common* as
   they can. Ask them to dig for commonalities that are not evident from
   physical appearance alone. To get them started, list these categories on
   newsprint:

   - Family background (e.g., we are both the oldest sibling)

   - Hobbies and interests (e.g., we like to read mysteries)

- Preferences (e.g., we dislike decaffeinated coffee)
- Life experiences (e.g., we have been to China)

3. After 10 minutes, request that pairs stop generating commonalities and pick two that might seem the most "intriguing" to the other participants. Then ask them to also make up a commonality that *in fact* is not true. Suggest that they try to "trick" others with their selections.

4. Reassemble the full group with partners seated together. Have each pair introduce themselves to the group and report the three commonalities they selected (two are in fact true and one is false). As they do so, invite other participants to speculate which commonality is false. Then ask pairs to reveal the truth.

5. Debrief the activity by asking for participants' feedback and reactions to the experience.

# Other Options

1. Every time you create new partners in the training program who will remain a pair for at least 30 minutes, have the pair search for three commonalities.

2. Have participants discover ways in which they are different rather than similar.

**Predictions: Making Guesses About Co-Participants**

┌─────────────── **Introductory Remarks** ───────────────┐

This activity is a fascinating way to help participants become acquainted with one another. It is also an interesting experience in first impressions. The twist in the activity is that participants do not begin by the standard introduction. Instead, other participants guess some details of the person being introduced.

└────────────────────────────────────────────────────────┘

## *Objectives*

- To learn not to make assumptions or leap to conclusions based on appearances.

- To experience self-disclosure as a way to get acquainted.

**Group Size:** any

**Time Required:** 20 minutes

**Materials:** none

## *Activity Flow*

1. Form subgroups of three or four participants (who are relative strangers to one another).

2. Tell the participants that their job is to predict how each person in their subgroup will answer certain questions you have prepared about him or her. The following are some all-purpose possibilities:

   - Where did you grow up?

   - What were you like as a child? As a student?

- Were your parents strict or lenient?

- What type of music do you enjoy?

- What are some of your favorite leisure activities?

- How many hours do you usually sleep nightly?

   *Note:* Other questions can be added or substituted, depending on the group you are leading.

3. Have subgroups begin by selecting one person as the first "subject." Urge participants to be as specific as possible in their predictions about the chosen person. Tell them not to be afraid of bold guesses! As the subgroup members guess, request that the "subject" give no indication as to the accuracy of the predictions. When the predictions about the "subject" are finished, the "subject" should then reveal the answer to each question about himself or herself.

4. Continue the same process with each person in the subgroup.

5. Debrief the exercise, using the following questions:

   - How well did you do with your predictions?

   - How did it feel to be the person about whom others made predictions?

   - What can you take away from this activity?

# Other Options

1. Create questions that require participants to make predictions about one another's views and beliefs (rather than factual details). Try to connect the questions to your training topic. For example, a question might be: What is a weakness I have in communicating clearly?

2. Eliminate the predictions. Instead, invite participants, one by one, to answer the questions immediately. Then ask subgroup members to reveal what facts about one another "surprised" them (based on their first impressions).

**Introductory Go-Arounds: Brief Self-Disclosures**

---

**Introductory Remarks**

This activity gives participants a safe way to disclose information about themselves. There are several different ways to conduct this activity. Choose what you like. I have found from this activity that the participants and I learn a lot about each other in a short period of time.

---

## Objectives

- To experience a safe way for people to get to know each other through self-disclosure.

- To set a norm of honest communication.

**Group Size:** up to fifteen participants

**Time Required:** 10 minutes

**Materials:** none

## Activity Flow

1. Prior to the session, create at least four sentence stems. (The larger the group, the fewer sentence stems you should use.) Here are some choices:

    - I am a member of _____.

    - I am happy to be here because _____.

    - One thing I remember from the last training I attended is _____.

- A favorite movie or book of mine is _____.
- As a child, I was _____.
- My dream job is to _____.
- My favorite leisure activity is _____.
- My attitude toward risk is _____.
- I wish that I could _____.

2. At the session, explain that a go-around is a rapid way for everyone to share something. You will use it as a way for participants to learn a lot about each other.

3. Go around the group asking each person to complete a sentence stem of your choosing. Pick as many sentence stems as time and energy warrant. Let any participant "pass" at any time in the go-arounds. If you have a very large group, divide into smaller groups and display the sentence stems. Have each group respond at its own pace.

4. Debrief the activity by asking: "What have you learned about us as a group?"

## Other Options

1. Have participants create their own sentence stems.

2. Instead of using a list of sentence stems, use a fishbowl format in which a small group discusses a question you provide (e.g., What is one thing you remember from the last training you attended?) and then is replaced by another group for a different question and so forth. Choose a different question for each fishbowl group.

# 6　What's in a Name? My Story

```
┌─────────────── Introductory Remarks ───────────────┐
│                                                     │
│  This activity is an unconventional way to learn    │
│  names and gain some connections to other           │
│  participants. It is based on the idea that most    │
│  people have a story to tell about their first      │
│  names: how they got the name and their fondness    │
│  or lack thereof for the name. The stories          │
│  participants tell each other begin a shared        │
│  experience that helps to create a new group        │
│  identity.                                          │
│                                                     │
└─────────────────────────────────────────────────────┘
```

## Objectives

- To learn names in an unusual way.
- To have an initial group-building experience.

**Group Size:** any

**Time Required:** 2 minutes per participant plus time for a short debriefing

**Materials:** none

## Activity Flow

1. Go around the group and ask participants to state their first names. After their names, ask them to tell the group some things about their names within 2 minutes. They can go into as much detail and background as time allows.

2. Include any of the following information:

   - Why he or she was given that name (if known)
   - Whether he or she ever had another name, such as a nickname

- Their feelings about their names

- Another name he or she would prefer

3. Some participants may have "stories" about their names. Permit the "stories" if they can stay within the time limit.

4. Debrief the exercise by asking participants how important their first names are to them.

## Other Options

1. Have other participants guess the answers to each question, followed by the participant's own answer.

2. Discuss any cultural factors related to their names.

# 2 COMMUNICATION

# Communication Tokens: An Awareness Exercise

## Introductory Remarks

There is a classic exercise in which participants can only speak when they relinquish a token before speaking. When any participant no longer has a token remaining from what was allocated, he or she can no longer speak. I took part in this activity many years ago. I still remember the experience because I used up all my tokens within a few minutes. My awareness of how impulsively I would speak in groups was naturally heightened. The present activity is based on this classic exercise with a few twists and turns of my own.

## *Objectives*

- To recognize one's own needs to talk in a group.
- To observe the strategies others use to handle communication restrictions.

**Group Size:** at least four

**Time Required:** 25 minutes

## *Materials*

- Three paper clips or pennies for each participant

## *Activity Flow*

1. Divide participants into groups of four to eight participants. Provide each participant with three paper clips or pennies to serve as "communication tokens."

2. Tell the groups that you would like them to discuss their feelings about poverty. The ideas can pertain to any aspect of poverty, including:

   - What constitutes poverty?

   - How much of poverty is a government problem?

   - What are the best ways to relieve poverty?

3. Explain that each group has up to 15 minutes for discussion. Inform participants that, whenever anyone wishes to speak, even to ask a question, that person has to give up one of his or her tokens. When a person no longer has tokens, he or she can no longer speak.

4. Begin the discussions. Observe the different ways participants handle the situation. Some will hoard their tokens. Some will relinquish them quickly.

5. When time is up, ask each subgroup to debrief its own experience. Questions for reflection include:

   - What did you do when you no longer had tokens? Did you find some other way to participate?

   - How did the use of tokens impact your own desire to speak?

   - How did it impact the process of the group?

6. Reconvene the entire group. Poll the group:

   - How many used up all three tokens?

   - What effect did the token rules have on you? On the entire group?

   - What can you take away from this activity? What would the consequences be if groups applied the lessons from the exercise?

# Other Options

1. Let the exercise be longer by giving each participant more tokens.

2. Continue the discussion without the use of tokens. What effect did that have on the group process?

**Direct Communication: You Write the Scripts**

---

**Introductory Remarks**

Good communicators are "straight-shooters" who make their feelings and intentions clear. They don't confuse or mislead others by hinting, avoiding, or beating around the bush. But for many of us, talking straight can be difficult. This activity eases participants into this challenging territory by allowing them to create their own role plays that demand direct communication.

---

## Objectives

- To understand the difference between direct and indirect talk.
- To practice direct communication in a safe environment.

**Group Size:** eight or more

**Time Required:** 30 minutes

**Materials:** none

## Activity Flow

1. Divide participants into quartets (if necessary, go up to five or six participants in a group).

2. Ask each quartet to agree on one of the three scenarios below:

   - Someone has taken credit for something you have done.
   - Someone has not kept a promise.
   - Someone continually disagrees with you.

3. Now ask each quartet to split into pairs. One pair is to devise a skit in which someone in the scenario is *not* a straight talker; he or she hides or hedges feelings, or comments on the other person's actions or motives, rather than his or her own. The other pair is to devise a skit in which the person *is* a straight talker. Use these as sample statements:

| **Direct Statement** | **Indirect Statements** |
| --- | --- |
| "I disagree." | "You've got to be kidding." |
| "I have a problem with that." | "Don't you think that. . . ." |
| "This ___isn't working for me." | "Maybe you should. . . ." |
| "I'm unsure about. . . ." | "Well, okay." |
| "I have some concerns here." | "Don't make it difficult." |
| "I can't do that." | "That's crazy." |

4. Ask the quartets to agree on the overall concept for their scripts, then polish them in pairs.

5. Ask each pair is to perform its skit for the other pair.

6. Reconvene the entire group. Obtain volunteers to re-do their skits for all the participants to observe.

7. Debrief the exercise. In particular, surface concerns about the perils of indirect communication. Offer to demonstrate how you would handle the situations more directly.

# Other Options

1. Discuss the reasons why people are reluctant to communicate directly. What are the risks? How serious are they? Then create a list of benefits for direct communication.

2. Conduct a discussion with this lead question:

   ▪ What are your ideas about how to communicate directly without creating anger or confusion?

**Explaining Something Complicated: Avoiding Information Dumps**

---

**┌─ Introductory Remarks ─┐**

It is especially challenging to communicate detailed information to someone else. "Dumping" information onto another person has many costs. The listener is overwhelmed. Moreover, communication becomes very one-way. This exercise is designed to test a person's ability to provide just enough information so that the listener feels communicated with rather than talked to. I often use it as a "real-world" follow-up to one of the classic one-way, two-way communication exercises, such as describing a diagram to someone with whom you sit back-to-back.

---

## Objectives

- To experience the problems involved in communicating detailed information.

- To learn five steps to include the listener when communicating complicated information.

**Group Size:** any

**Time Required:** 30 minutes

## Materials

- One copy of the Including the Listener handout for each participant

- One copy of the Five Tips to Include the Listener handout for each participant

## *Activity Flow*

1. Pair up participants. Distribute the Including the Listener handout.

2. In each pair, ask each person to choose a topic (using the handout as a guide) to communicate to his or her partner. Make sure that a topic is selected that the partner knows little about. Provide time for each member of the pair to explain the topic chosen.

3. Distribute the Five Tips to Include the Listener handout. Invite pairs to debrief the exercise as per suggestions on the handout. Ask: "How does each tip help you to include the listener?"

4. Reconvene the entire group. Ask them to share steps that their "communication partners" used effectively. Have them refer to the Five Tips to Include the Listener handout.

5. Discuss the handout, clarifying key points. Then obtain examples of when each tip was relevant in the exercise.

## Other Options ——————————————————————

1. Create pairs. Have each pair select any of the following:

   - Travel directions to one's home or place of work

   - Any game, such as chess, football, or poker

   - The process of bankruptcy

   Using the Five Tips to Include the Listener handout as a guide, ask each pair to brainstorm how they would communicate their selection effectively to someone with little prior knowledge of the subject.

2. Evaluate how any currently popular TV game show can be explained to someone who has never viewed it before.

# *Including the Listener*

*Instructions;* Take turns explaining one of the following topics to your partner. Choose a topic about which you have some knowledge, but your partner does not:

- The benefits of a product or service (e.g., a new drug)
- The features of a product or service (e.g., new operating system)
- Understanding a procedure (e.g., safe handling of dangerous equipment)
- The difference between a _____ and a _____ (e.g., HMO/PPO or PC/MAC)
- Tips for _____ (e.g., searching the web)
- (Supply your own)

# *Five Tips to Include the Listener*

1. Orient the listener first.

2. Don't overload the listener with information. Use key points.

3. Feed information in chunks.

4. Use references the listener readily understands.

5. Allow space and encourage the listener to speak or ask questions.

# 10 Obtaining Participation: Using Different Formats

---
**Introductory Remarks**

Most people lead discussions using what I call an "open mike." Participants speak up on their own when they have something to say, with or without raising hands, so that the discussion leader knows who wants to speak. I developed the tool *10 Formats for Group Discussion* several years ago to broaden the ways in which people can have discussions in groups. Here participants have the opportunity to clarify the options and select those options that would work for them to avoid the open-mike format.

---

## Objectives

- To identify ten alternative ways to format a group discussion.
- To practice the ten formats.

**Group Size:** up to twenty-four participants

**Time Required:** 40 minutes

## Materials

- One copy of the Ten Formats for Group Discussion handout for each participant

# *Activity Flow*

1. Invite the participants to read the Ten Formats handout and to identify formats for obtaining participation they have used and not used.

2. Poll the total group. Which have they used in the past?

3. Count off the participants by three. Invite the "1's" to form a circle and have the remaining participants form a circle surrounding them [resulting in two concentric circles]. Ask the "1's" this question: "*What* experience do you have using any of these techniques?" Next, invite the "2's" to replace the "1's" in the inner circle, and ask them, "*When* would you use each of these methods? What are their relative advantages and disadvantages?" Finally, invite the "3's" to replace the "2's" and ask, "What are *your reactions* to using these methods in the future as ways of obtaining participation?"

4. Reconvene the entire group. Note that you just used a "fishbowl" technique to obtain everyone's participation. Inquire what other methods you might have employed (referring to the Ten Formats handout). Obtain answers.

5. Inform the group that you would like them to practice different formats. Divide participants into groups of six or eight members.

6. In each group, obtain a volunteer facilitator. Explain that he or she is about to conduct a discussion on people's views of "blended learning." Questions to be addressed include:

   - What experiences have you had as a participant or facilitator using blended learning?

   - What are your personal feelings about blended learning? What works? What doesn't?

7. Each facilitator should consult his or her group about the format that could be used for the discussion on blended learning and reach a decision within a couple of minutes.

8. Each group proceeds with its discussion.

9. Stop after 10 or 15 minutes. Reconvene the entire group. Ask each facilitator to form a panel (one of the formats) to share what format his or her group experienced and what the effect was.

## Other Options ────────────────────────────

1. Announce a discussion topic. Ask participants to brainstorm how they might combine two of the ten formats (for example, subgroup discussion followed by a panel discussion).

2. Choose two formats and compare them. Discuss the advantages and disadvantages of each.

# *Ten Formats for Group Discussion*

1. ***Open discussion.*** Ask a question and open it up to the entire group without any further structuring. Use open discussion when you are certain that several participants want to participate. Its voluntary quality is also appealing. Don't overuse this method. If you do, you will limit participants to those who are comfortable about raising their hands. If you have a very participative group and are worried that the discussion might be too lengthy, say beforehand, "I'd like to ask four or five participants to share. . . ." If you are worried that few people will volunteer, say, "How many of you can tell us . . .?" rather than "Who can tell us . . .?"

2. ***Response cards.*** Pass out index cards and request anonymous answers to your questions. Use response cards to save time, to provide anonymity for personally threatening self-disclosures, or to make it easier for shy people to contribute. The need to state yourself concisely on a card is another advantage of this method. Say, "For this discussion, I would like you to write down your thoughts first before we talk together any further." Have the index cards passed around the group or have them returned to you to be read at a later point. Be careful to make your questions clear, and encourage brief, legible responses.

3. ***Polling.*** Verbally poll all participants or provide a questionnaire that is filled out and tallied on the spot. Use polling to obtain data quickly and in a quantifiable form. Pose questions that call for a clear-cut answer such as "I agree" or "That's true." Ask participants to raise their hands when the responses they agree with are given. In place of raising their hands, you can ask them to hold up response cards that represent their choices (for example, a yellow card might indicate "false") or place a color-coded dot on a designated area of a large form such as a chart or newsprint. If you use a questionnaire, make it short and easy to tally immediately.

4. ***Subgroup discussions.*** Form participants into subgroups of three or more to share and record information. Use subgroup discussions when you have sufficient time to process questions and issues. This is one of the key methods for obtaining everyone's participation. You can assign people to subgroups randomly (for example, by counting off) or purposively (for example, by forming an all-female group). Pose a question for discussion

or give the subgroup a task or assignment to complete. It is often helpful to designate group roles such as facilitator, timekeeper, recorder, or presenter and to obtain volunteers or assign members to fill them. Make sure that participants are in face-to-face contact with each other. Try to separate subgroups so that they do not disturb each other.

5. *Partners*. Form participants into pairs and instruct them to work on tasks or discuss key questions. Use partners when you want to involve everybody but do not have enough time for small group discussion. A pair is a good group configuration for developing a long-term supportive relationship and/or for working on complex activities that would not lend themselves to larger group configurations. Pair up participants either by physical proximity or by a wish to put certain participants together. Often, it is not necessary to move chairs to create pair activities. You can ask pairs to do many things, such as reading and discussing a short written document together, developing or responding to a question, or comparing their results to those on some activity they performed previously on an independent basis. Give instructions such as, "Read this handout together and discuss it. Come up with examples or applications of what you are reading," "Create a question you both have about this topic," "Discuss together your response to the following question," or "Compare your results on this survey. How are you alike or different?"

6. *Go-arounds*. Go around the group and obtain short responses to key questions. Use this method when you want to obtain something quickly from each participant. Sentence stems (for example, "One thing that makes a manager effective is. . . .") are useful in conducting go-arounds. Invite participants to "pass" when they wish. Avoid repetition, if you wish, by asking each participant for a new contribution to the process. If the group is large, create a smaller go-around group by obtaining short responses from one side of the room, from people who are wearing glasses, or from some other smaller sample.

7. *Games*. Use popular games or quiz game formats to elicit participants' ideas or knowledge. Use games to stimulate energy and involvement. Virtually any game can be adapted for training purposes, including basketball, Bingo, darts, Jeopardy, poker, Family Feud, Pictionary, Wheel of Fortune, bowling, Scrabble, soccer, and crossword puzzles. Be sure that

the game requires everyone's participation and make the instructions crystal clear.

8. ***Calling on the next speaker.*** Ask participants to raise their hands when they want to share their views and ask the present speaker in the group, not the leader, to call on the next speaker. Say, "For this discussion, I would like you to call on each other rather than having me select who is to speak next. When you have finished speaking, look around to see whose hands are raised and call on someone." (Do not allow participants to call on people who have not indicated a desire to participate.) Use calling on the next speaker when you are sure that there is a lot of interest in the discussion or activity and you wish to promote participant interaction. When you wish to resume as moderator, inform the group that you are changing back to the regular format.

9. ***Panels.*** Invite a small number of participants to present their views in front of the entire group. Use panels when time permits to have a focused, serious response to your questions. Rotate panelists to increase participation. An informal panel can be created by asking for the views of a designated number of participants who remain in their seats. Serve as panel moderator or invite a participant to perform this role.

10. ***Fishbowls.*** Ask a portion of the group to form a discussion circle and have the remaining participants form a listening circle around them. Use a fishbowl to help bring focus to large group discussions. Although it is time-consuming, this is the best method for combining the virtues of both large and small group discussion. Bring new groups into the inner circle to continue the discussion. You can do this by obtaining new volunteers or assigning participants to be discussants. As a variation of concentric circles, you can have participants remain seated at a table and invite different table groups or parts of a table group to be the discussants as the others listen.

# 3 ASSERTIVE BEHAVIOR

**Concerns About Confronting Employees: Overcoming the Anxiety**

---

**———Introductory Remarks———**

Confronting employees raises a lot of concerns. A manager may be worried about upsetting the employee or showing his or her own displeasure. As a result, the manager may want to "let things go" to see whether his or her concerns subside. In this activity, participants have an opportunity to examine these concerns through visualization and role play. Most skills, especially assertion skills, should not be taught without dealing with the emotional concerns of the people you are training. For this reason, I make it a practice of using an activity such as the following before plunging into skill-building.

---

## Objectives

- To identify feelings of anxiety about the prospect of confronting employees.

- To select ways to manage those emotions effectively.

**Group Size:** at least ten participants.

**Time Required:** 30 minutes

# *Materials*

- One copy of the Role Playing a Counseling Situation handout for each participant

# *Activity Flow*

1. Point out that a situation would not call for confronting an employee unless there is some dissatisfaction. Confronting employees is especially difficult when you anticipate some resistance. Otherwise, it would be a straightforward performance feedback situation.

2. Pair up participants and ask each partner to think of an employee whose performance needs some improvement. Ask each person to choose a specific behavior he or she would like to see changed. Speaking slowly as if you were conducting a mental imagery exercise, direct each participant to visualize herself/himself moments *before* confronting that employee about poor performance. Ask participants to then identify some of their concerns about the upcoming encounter. Suggest some possibilities:

   - You're concerned about upsetting the employee.

   - You feel annoyed and even a little bit angry and are concerned that it will show.

   - You wish you could avoid the encounter because you are concerned that the employee will be upset with you.

   - You'd rather let things go because once you start with this employee, you'll have to invest a lot of time.

   Request that participants share their situations and concerns with their partners. Note that few people are immune to such concerns.

3. Indicate that the more confident one is in her or his ability to confront and counsel employees, the less she or he will feel concerns such as those above.

4. In the same pairs, conduct the role playing situation described in the handout, with one person as Jo/Joe and the other as Chris. The "confronter" should do the best he or she can in being assertive.

5. Begin the debriefing of the role play by asking two participants who portrayed the employee, Jo/Joe, to "brag" about the assertive skills of their manager, Chris.

6. Ask the entire group for ideas on how to lessen concerns about asserting themselves with others and to increase their confidence to handle the situations.

Include any of the following suggestions if not otherwise stated by the participants:

- Before you approach the employee, be clear about the specific behaviors you are concerned about and what you expect instead.

- Don't rush your remarks. Take pauses to slow yourself down.

- Be open to resistance. Don't dominate the discussion. Invite the employee to share his or her take on the situation.

- Support the idea that you are concerned about the "deed," not the "doer." Focus on behavior, not personality.

- Think about the value of "getting your concerns on the table" rather than withholding them. Be conscious of the fact that it is unfair to the employee to not learn about your concerns.

# Other Options ─────────────────────

1. Have small groups create skits in which concerns about confronting an employee are not recognized and prepared for.

2. Interview willing participants to uncover underlying concerns about confronting others.

# *Role Playing a Counseling Situation*

## *Manager's Role: Chris*

You have been with the company for five years and have been manager of your unit since last year. Currently, you are managing ten employees and your unit has gone through some changes. Hence, several of your employees are new to the organization. You have had several meetings with your employees trying to build up a team atmosphere. Overall, you have been successful.

Jo (or Joe) has worked for you for several years and is a terrific technical expert. You recently have given her a chance as a project leader on an important data conversion project but now are worried about her interpersonal skills. Jo tends to jump to conclusions, interrupts people, and is impatient. You have asked Jo to see you, at which time you want to discuss your concerns.

## *Employee's Role: Jo/Joe*

You have recently become the project leader on a data conversion project that has been a challenge even for you, the most competent of technical data processing people. You are aware that Chris, your manager, is very pleased with your technical accomplishments on this conversion. However, you have been having difficulty with the team and Chris has asked to see you.

## 12 Assertive Starters: Ways to Begin an Assertive Message

### Introductory Remarks

This activity provides choices about how to begin an assertive message. Giving people concrete options helps them to become clearer as to how insistent they want the message to be and provides them with direction about how to express themselves confidently. I have found that participants appreciate the list of starters provided in the activity.

## Objectives

- To help participants formulate an assertive message.

- To experience the effect of different starting phrases.

**Group Size:** any

**Time Required:** 20 to 25 minutes

## Materials

- One copy of the Assertive Starters handout for each participant

# *Activity Flow*

1. Explain to participants that starting off well when communicating what you want or don't want from others is very important. It sets the tone of your encounter. There are many phrases to use to begin the communication. Some are more forceful, while some are less so. It's best to base your choice on how you want to address the other person.

2. You can communicate your position, using phrases as varied as:

   - I would appreciate it if you . . . (call me first thing in the morning).
   - I will not . . . (be able to come to the meeting).
   - It would be great if you . . . (could give me a day's notice).
   - I will have to . . . (turn down your request).
   - Please . . . (tell me when you are ready for the next assignment).
   - I would prefer that you . . . (get assistance from someone with more free time).
   - It works best for me if . . . (you put it in writing).
   - I've decided not to . . . (be on the committee).

3. Distribute the Assertive Starters handout and ask participants to complete it.

4. Pair up participants. Have each take a turn describing the person with whom he or she would like to be more assertive in one or more situations of his or her choosing. Then each should explain why he or she chose the phrase he or she did. For example, one partner may be open to compromise and therefore choose a phrase that is more benign than others.

5. Next, ask pairs to actually say the starting sentences to their partners as if they were the people being addressed. They should also state a brief reason for the statement. Invite the partners to share how they experienced the starting sentence (and the reason).

6. Debrief the experience with the entire group. How useful did they find the list of phrases? Some of the starters are strongly worded, while others are more gentle. When would they use each?

## Other Options

1. Have the group brainstorm a list of undesirable ways to begin an assertive encounter. Include both timid and off-putting phrases.

2. Have participants rate the phrases in terms of their forcefulness. Then have them choose situations in which they would select each one.

# *Assertive Starters*

1. Select a person (or category of people) with whom you would like to be more assertive. _____

2. Choose at least three phrases from the list below to begin a conversation with that person and complete the entire sentence.

   I would appreciate it if you _____.

   I will not _____.

   It would be great if you _____.

   I will have to _____.

   Please _____.

   I would prefer that you _____.

   It works best for me if _____.

   I've decided not to _____.

# on-Verbal Persuasion: Assessing
# ts Impact

## Introductory Remarks

The usual assumption is that we need to use words to convey intent. This overlooks the power of nonverbal communication. The following is what I call "an exaggerated exercise." What participants do is extreme. In real life, one would modify the behavior as appropriate to the situation. However, taking the behavior to the extreme allows the participant to get in touch with it more vividly.

## *Objectives*

- To experience the use of nonverbal communication as a powerful way to influence someone else.

- To learn which nonverbal behaviors are effective when you want to be persuasive.

**Group Size:** any

**Time Required:** 20 minutes

**Materials:** none

## *Activity Flow*

1. Explain that the following exercise tests participants' skill at being persuasive without words.

2. Pair up participants. In each pair, there will be a persuader and a resister. Each member of the pair will experience both roles.

3. Request the first resister in each pair to get up and walk somewhere in the room in which he or she can be alone. Tell the resister not to talk with other resisters and to stay in one spot. They may talk to their persuader, with the intent of resisting him or her.

4. After the resister is settled, give the (seated) persuaders the following instructions: "When you are ready, go to your resister and, *without talking*, do whatever you can to urge him or her to return to his or her seat."

   After 5 minutes (or when all resisters have returned to their seats), have partners reverse roles and repeat the same process with the same directions.

5. Reconvene the entire group. Post possible actions the persuader may have used:

   - Offered money

   - Done something pleasant, such as providing a backrub

   - Dragged the resister back to his or her seat

6. Ask participants to share what nonverbal behaviors their persuaders used from the posted list or anything else they did.

7. Debrief the experience with the following questions:

   - How confident did you feel with the nonverbals you used?

   - What did you do that helped you to stay calm and persistent?

   - What nonverbals were you surprised by?

   - What are you taking away from this exercise?

# Other Options

1. Have participants brainstorm nonverbal behaviors that express disapproval, that express confidence, and that express nonassertiveness. For fun, have each person stand up and do something from the lists. No one, however, can repeat what someone else has done.

2. List three aspects of nonverbal communication: voice tone, posture, and eye contact. Have participants take turns demonstrating assertive and nonassertive ways to use each.

# Refusing Unwanted Requests: Practicing Saying No

## Introductory Remarks

A basic task when asserting needs is to be able to refuse unwanted requests. This activity first requires the identification of situations in which the participants want to say no. This is followed by exercises to practice saying no. In my experience, participants are very liberated by this activity. They gain permission to refuse to do things that previously they have not been able to refuse. This process emboldens them to be able to refuse unwanted requests in their real lives.

## *Objectives*

- To identify personal examples of wanting to say no.
- To experience saying no and evaluating its effect.

**Group Size:** any

**Time Required:** 30 to 40 minutes

## *Materials*

- One copy of the When I Want to Say No handout for each participant
- One container for slips of paper (a hat or bag)
- Slips of paper with situations written on them (see Step 5)

# *Activity Flow*

1. Explain that it is especially helpful to take a stand first on matters when people want something from you, rather than the other way around. That's only possible when you have more confidence to say "no" to someone's request rather than to make a successful request of others.

2. Distribute the When I Want to Say No handout. Ask participants to write down a list of possible "no's" they would like to express right now in their lives. Next ask participants to read over their lists.

3. Pair up participants. Request that each person select two items from his or her list and share with his or her partner any background information relevant to the circumstances of each item.

4. Now give pairs an opportunity to communicate their wishes in both situations to their partners as if they were the actual persons being addressed. Tell them to feel free to embellish their messages with brief rationales.

5. Reconvene the entire group. Put in a hat or any other container several slips of paper containing a wish to say no. Here are many situations. Add more of your own.

   ▪ You don't want to attend a meeting you are expected to attend because you have a competing obligation.

   ▪ You don't want to write a letter of recommendation because you don't know enough about the performance of the requester.

   ▪ You don't want to help someone with a PowerPoint presentation because you have been asked many times before.

   ▪ You don't want to give someone a raise because his or her current performance, while good, is not meritorious.

   ▪ You don't want to read an early draft of a report because you don't have the time.

   ▪ You don't want to be part of a team whose project lies outside your expertise.

   ▪ You don't want to work over the weekend on an important assignment because your family comes first.

6. Obtain as many volunteers as time will allow to role play one of the situations. Invite each volunteer to select a fellow participant to play the role of the person being addressed. That person is allowed to "push back" after the refuser states his or her wish.

7. Debrief the role plays. Questions to ask include:

   ■ How did it feel to be the refuser?

   ■ How did it feel to be the person being refused?

   ■ What was helpful in your role as refuser?

8. Invite participants to each select a "refusal" that they will express in the coming week.

## Other Options

1. Tell participants about the popular book entitled *When I Say No, I Feel Guilty.* Invite participants to share personal stories of when this title fit for them.

2. Ask participants to rate each item on their lists, using the following:

   ■ Insistent

   ■ Willing to provide other options

   ■ Open to doing what the other person wants one time only

# *When I Want to Say No*

I would like to say "no" when:

1. _____

2. _____

3. _____

4. _____

5. _____

6. _____

# **15** Stating Complaints and Requesting Change: Skill Practice

## ──────────── Introductory Remarks ────────────

Many people avoid assertive communication by either hinting at or attributing motive. If you want your participants to speak up rather than avoid direct talk and want them to do so without putting another person down, this skill practice exercise might be just what you're looking for.

## *Objectives*

- To distinguish assertive behavior from nonassertive behavior.

- To practice assertive ways to state complaints and request change.

**Group Size:** any

**Time Required:** 30 minutes

**Materials:** none

## *Activity Flow*

1. Point out that full-blown conflicts can be avoided in relationships by being assertive up-front.

2. Make these key points:

   - When you have a complaint with another person, hinting rarely influences her or him to do something about it.

- Also, attacking another person only makes her or him defensive.

- The most effective action is to directly state your complaint *in behavioral terms* (that describe what the other person specifically *does*, not his or her personal attributes) and directly *request* something be done about it.

3. Ask participants to give examples of complaints that are not behavioral and do not contain a request. Examples might include:

   - "You've been very rude lately."

   - "Why don't you listen for a change!?"

   - "I think you want to put words in my mouth."

   - "Don't you think you could be more positive?"

4. Demonstrate an effective way of stating complaints and requesting change, using examples appropriate to your training group. Below is an example of a script:

   "Jim, I have a complaint. You are late to most of our meetings. I'd appreciate it if you would commit yourself to coming on time. Can you agree to that?"

5. Ask participants to form pairs and to each select one complaint he or she has with another person in the workplace. Using their partners in the imaginary role of the other person, have each participant practice stating a concrete complaint and making a request for change. After each performance, have partners give each other feedback.

6. Point out that it may help to communicate friendly intentions by *expressing appreciations* before stating complaints and *acknowledging your role in the situation* before requesting change. Give a demonstration using this sample script as a guide:

   "Jim, I've appreciated your contributions to our team. (pause) I do have one complaint. You are late to most of our meetings. I recognize that I haven't told you before that this upsets me, but I would like you to commit yourself to coming on time. Can you agree to that?"

7. Invite pairs to practice these added steps with each other using the same complaint. Direct them now, in their roles as the other person, to

respond defensively to the complaint and request for change by "cross-complaining" (for example, "Don't you think that you waste time on chitchat at the start of meetings?"). This means bringing up one's own complaint. Urge participants to figure out how to respond.

8.  After the role plays are finished, invite some participants to "brag" to the full group about how their partners effectively responded to the cross-complaining. If not stated, include any of these points:

    ■ Don't get sidetracked. Repeat your point. Provide further explanation but keep it brief. Don't get defensive or caught up in a power struggle or blow your cool.

    ■ Acknowledge that you heard the "counter-argument." Share where you think it may be true with a phrase such as: "That may be."

9.  Discuss other defensive behaviors that might occur, such as arguing, acting insulted, making excuses, and so forth. Utilize the life experiences of participants by appealing to their ideas for dealing with each of these moves.

# Other Options

1.  Divide participants into groups of four. Each group of four will create and act out skits that show the contrast between complaints that are "nonassertive" (only hint), "aggressive" (attacking), and "assertive" (direct but not hostile). Two members will perform the "nonassertive" or "aggressive" demonstration, after which the other two members will perform the "assertive" demonstration.

2.  If your training will run multiple sessions, give each participant the responsibility to assert a complaint and request change with someone back on the job. At the beginning of the next session, obtain feedback about what people did and what they took away from their experience when applying the skill in "real" time.

# 4 INFLUENCING OTHERS

# 16 Alligator River: Looking at People with Different Glasses

### ——————Introductory Remarks——————

During this exercise, participants are asked to respond to a fictional story about the plight of two lovers who are separated from each other by a river infested with alligators. Participants are asked to rate four characters to whom one lover turns in order to figure out how to cross the river to her partner. What surprises participants is that they differ in their responses to these four characters. This is an experience of understanding how selective perception influences attitudes about people.

## Objectives

- To appreciate that people see others from different perspectives.

- To witness the effects on mutual understanding when people are in a debate mode.

- To understand how one's assumptions affect perceptions.

**Group Size:** any size
**Time Required:** 45 to 60 minutes

## Materials

- A copy of the Alligator River handout for each participant

- Flip chart and markers

- (Optional) Sunglasses with different tints—one rosy and one dark

# *Activity Flow*

1. Tell participants the story on the handout at the end of this activity.

2. Distribute the Alligator River handout, and ask participants to review the story you just told them.

3. Instruct participants to rank the characters on a 1 to 4 scale in terms of how offensive they found them, with 1 being the most offensive and 4 the least.

4. Identify one participant who sees each of the four characters as the most offensive. (If a character is not chosen as the most offensive by any of the participants, inquire whether that character was a second choice for anyone.) Instruct these four individuals to sit in front of the entire group and to advocate for their own views on the characters. Tell them not to fear a heated exchange. Treat it like a debate. After 10 minutes, stop the discussion.

5. Ask: "As you tried to win people over, did you really try to understand where they were coming from?" Obtain responses, first from the four discussants and then from the rest of the group.

6. Put on a pair of rosy sunglasses (optional).

7. Say: "There are two points to this exercise. One is that we all see the world through our own glasses. Each character is viewed a little differently by each of us. Some of us may see them through rosy glasses, in mostly positive terms, while others wear darker lenses and see them more negatively." [Change glasses to a darker color.] "The more we can recognize the glasses others see the world through, the better we can understand their perspectives and preferences. The second point is that, when we get into a debate or conflict mode (as I instructed you to do), we don't usually put much effort into suspending judgment and reflecting on the nuances of the situation."

8. Say: "Let's look at some questions to help you understand the glasses others were wearing":

   - How old is Abigail?

   - How long will it take for the bridge to be replaced?

   - Did Sinbad force Abigail to give him her gold locket?

- Why did Ivan not want to be involved?

- What was Gregory doing while Abigail was trying to get across Alligator River?

9. Discuss each of the questions. Observe whether the differing answers to these questions affected the positions of the four participants.

10. Say: "It's relatively easy to listen when there's no conflict, but attempts to understand often are discarded when the heat is on between people."

11. Ask: "What are some examples of times when the heat is on in your life?"

12. Discuss responses. Ask: "What are some of the 'glasses' people see the world through?" Chart participants' answers.

13. Say: "When we try to list the sources of people's different perspectives on the world, the list can get quite long. Some of the major sources of difference, though, include age, gender, and culture. Let's try a quick experiment. Who thinks he or she might be the youngest person in the room?" Check the candidates' ages to identify the youngest. Ask: "Who's willing to admit to perhaps being the oldest?" Identify the oldest.

14. Instruct the youngest and oldest participants to come to the front of the room. Ask: "What might be some of the major differences in how these two look at the world? What are the different glasses they wear?" Obtain responses, asking the two at the front to verify participants' guesses. Thank the two for their help.

15. Observe the ratio of men to women in the room.

16. Say: "Let's take a small risk here. We're not looking to stereotype, but we know there are differences between men and women. Let's explore what some of those different perspectives might be." Ask the women: "How do you think the guys feel about sharing their innermost feelings?" Ask the men to comment on the women's responses.

17. Ask the men: "How do you think the women might see the work world differently than you do?" Ask the women to comment on their responses.

18. Ask: "How difficult do you find it to 'walk in the other person's shoes' when the person is a different gender?" Briefly discuss responses.

19. Ask: "How many of you think that the world really looks different to people of different cultural backgrounds? What are some examples?" Discuss participants' examples.

20. Say: "Here's a quick demonstration of how our culture affects our view of the world. When you were a child, how did your family treat a cold?"

21. Record participants' responses (chicken soup, Vicks, tea with lemon) on a flip chart. Ask: "Do you see some cultural differences in this list?"

22. Say: "Sometimes, we're not all that aware that our cultural heritage is another kind of 'glasses' we wear, or that other people's glasses give them a very different view. But making the effort to consider factors like these can help us understand others."

23. Wrap up by summarizing the discussion on a flip chart and asking participants how they can take what they have learned back to their workplaces.

# Other Options

1. Conduct the same exercise as above. Instead of setting up a conflict among four participants who favor each of the four characters, create subgroups of three to five people and ask them to come to a consensus on the ranking.

2. Go directly into a discussion of how culture, gender, and age affect the values and preferences of people. Include comparisons such as:

   - Being spontaneous versus being careful
   - Being social versus being private
   - Being emotional versus being analytic
   - Being "take charge" versus being responsive
   - Being competitive versus being collaborative
   - Being opinionated versus being inquiring
   - Being intense versus being private
   - Being confronting versus being avoiding
   - Being self-oriented versus being group-oriented
   - Being loose versus being rule-oriented

# *Alligator River*

Once upon a time, there was a woman named Abigail who was in love with a man named Gregory. Gregory lived on one shore of the river. Abigail lived on the opposite shore of the river. The river that separated the two lovers was teeming with alligators. Abigail wanted to cross the river to be with Gregory.

Unfortunately, the bridge had been washed out. So she went to ask Sinbad, a riverboat captain, to take her across. He said he would be glad to if she would give him the gold locket she was wearing. (The locket originally belonged to Gregory's grandmother. Gregory had given it to Abigail.) She promptly refused and went to a friend named Ivan to explain her plight. Ivan did not want to be involved in the situation at all. Abigail felt that her only alternative was to give Sinbad the locket. Sinbad fulfilled his promise to Abigail and delivered her into the arms of Gregory. When Abigail told Gregory about giving Sinbad the locket in order to cross the river, Gregory cast her aside with disdain.

*Source:* Adapted from Simon, Howe, and Kirshenbaum, 1995, pp. 291–292.

# 17 Question First: The Best Way to Overcome Resistance

## Introductory Remarks

This exercise shows that exclusively advocating an idea, recommendation, or product to someone who is resistant is usually an act of futility. A volunteer participant plays the role of someone who is resistant to the suggestion of a radical change in diet. As the facilitator, you will try to persuade the resistor by giving a nonstop pitch for the radical dietary change. Because the persuader does not inquire about the concerns and wishes of the resistor, the persuasion effort will not be successful. As facilitator, you will shift to a questioning approach to show how one would have a better chance of succeeding by asking questions and listening to the answers.

## *Objectives*

- To demonstrate the futility of persuasion efforts without asking questions.

- To practice asking questions to uncover another person's concerns and needs.

**Group Size:** unlimited

**Time Required:** 20 to 30 minutes

**Materials:** none

# *Activity Flow*

1.  Identify participants who do not eat three to five fruits and three to five vegetables daily. Request a volunteer from this group who is willing to listen and respond to your attempt to persuade him or her to adopt this daily practice.

2.  Explain to the rest of participants that you are going to attempt to persuade the person (who should be very resistant) to adopt your point of view that eating three to five fruits and vegetables daily is critical to one's health and well-being. Tell them that you will be operating under a specific constraint in your efforts and ask them to see whether they can figure out what it is. (The constraint is that you will not be allowed to ask the person any questions.)

3.  Begin. Present your most persuasive arguments. Be sure not to ask any questions. Do all the talking. Stop the role play when appropriate. Ask participants (including the role-playing resistor) to give their feedback on your persuasion efforts. See whether anyone can identify what your particular constraint was. (It is quite likely that someone will notice that the conversation was one-way because you never asked a question.)

4.  Ask: "What questions could I have asked to better understand the person I was trying to convince?" Keep the questions flowing as long as possible.

5.  Say: "We often try to convince people of something without finding out their needs, concerns, and objections. With this information, we are in a better position to decide how the other person's objections might be overcome."

6.  Briefly do a re-take of the role play, showing how it would have been different if you had asked relevant questions. (Utilize as many of the questions provided by the rest of group as possible.) Obtain reactions to the difference.

7.  Point out that responses to the questions provide valuable information to adjust how you could be persuasive. Also point out the positive effect of the questions on the resistor, who now feels "listened to" rather than "talked at."

8.  End with the suggestion that the more eager you are to win over a resistor, the more resistant he or she might be. It's better to be open to the resistance than to fight it.

9. Do a final debriefing. End with this question:

"How can we apply this experience to the work we do with others?" (Specifically, how can we be more effective if we are open to resistance rather than blocking it?)

# Other Options

1. Divide participants into pairs. Assign one the role of persuader and the other the role of resistor. Identify a recommendation that the persuader endorses from the list below but the resistor is against (for whatever reason):

   - Going on a trip to China (or substitute any other location)
   - Subscribing to Netflix
   - Meditating daily
   - Changing from a PC to a Mac
   - Taking a yoga class
   - Limiting TV to no more than one hour per week
   - Joining Facebook
   - Walking one mile a day

   Encourage the persuader to frequently ask questions. Obtain reactions to the experience.

2. Identify ways to soften resistance such as:

   - Trying something once
   - Urging the person to consider a small, initial action rather than adopting your entire recommendation
   - Inviting the person to read something that supports your recommendation

   Now ask participants to apply one of these ideas to a situation they face with resistors.

# 18 Influencing Others: Four Role-Play Scenarios

## ———Introductory Remarks———

In this activity, participants are given some guidance about how to best influence someone who is resistant to one's advice. Next, they practice their influence skills in four situations. The role-play situations are challenging and act as a good test of one's ability to avoid using pressure tactics to get results.

## *Objectives*

- To understand the difference between pressure and influence.
- To practice influencing skills.

**Group Size:** any size

**Time Required:** 30 minutes

## *Materials*

- One copy of the Four Role-Play Scenarios handout for each participant

## *Activity Flow*

1. Explain that there is a difference between pressure and influence. Strongly persuading someone to follow your suggestions or recommendations using pressure can be accomplished in a variety of ways:

- Using forceful arguments to convince the other person until he or she agrees

- Indicating your annoyance or displeasure about the other person's resistance to your advice

- Suggesting or even threatening consequences if the person fails to comply

Trying to influence other people to adopt your advice implies that you are hoping to get them to come to their own decisions. This happens when you:

- Try to understand the other person's concerns and preferences

- Appeal to the benefits the other person will obtain from your advice

- Give the other person time to mull over your proposals

2. Distribute the Four Role-Play Scenarios handout. Review the list of four situations from the handout.

3. Pair up participants. Designate one partner in each pair as Person A and the other partner as Person B. Person B's role is to be somewhat defensive and resistant until the influencer is so effective that further resistance is not necessary. Each partner will have a chance to play each role twice, with Person A as the influencer in Situations 1 and 3 and Person B as the influencer in Situations 2 and 4. Participants should use the opportunity to practice the influence skills that have been discussed so far. Tell the participants they have up to 5 minutes for each situation

4. As the pairs complete each role play, explain that the person being influenced should provide feedback to the influencer about that person's influencing skills. In addition, the influencers should process their own experiences. Ask: "How difficult was playing the influencer? Did you lapse into applying pressure?"

5. Debrief the activity by asking the group: "What are some effective ways to overcome resistance you can use in the future?"

# Other Options ──────────────────────

1. Instead of simultaneous role plays in pairs, invite participants to volunteer to be the influencer or the resistor and perform each role play in front of the entire group. Or use either of the following formats:

   - *Rotational role playing.* Actors in front of the group can be rotated, usually by interrupting the role play in progress and replacing one or more of the actors.

   - *Use of different actors.* More than one actor can be recruited to role play the same situation in its entirety. This allows the group to observe more than one style or approach.

2. Discuss rather than role play the four situations. Encourage participants to be as specific as possible in describing how they would handle each one. Ask for any specific wording they would use.

# *Four Role-Play Scenarios*

1. You have been trying to convince a person who reports to you to take more initiative. That may include actions such as:

   - Suggesting a better way to do something

   - When possible, undertaking a small project without waiting to be assigned to do it

   - Giving you feedback about your behavior as a manager

   Until now, the person has been reluctant to do this. Try to change his or her mind.

2. You want your busy boss to give you performance feedback more frequently. He or she feels that you are doing a great job and don't need the extra feedback. Your boss is also overwhelmed with his or her own responsibilities. See whether you can get the boss to commit him- or herself to what you want.

3. Someone on your team disagrees with your insistence that no important decisions are to be made by individuals unless they are checked out with everyone else on the team. Persuade him or her to agree with you.

4. One of your customers continues to use a service or product from another provider that you know is inferior to your own. Convince him or her to give you the business.

# 19  Getting Your Foot in the Door: Avoiding Rejection

---
## Introductory Remarks
---

When you encounter strong resistance to your attempts
to persuade someone else, instead of pushing further
or giving up, it helps to encourage the person to take
a small step in the direction you want him or her to
go. This is often called "getting a foot in the door" (as
opposed to "getting the door in the face!"). In this
activity, four "getting your foot in the door" strategies are
presented. Learning and applying these strategies opens
up participants' imaginations about what to do when the
people they are trying to influence shut down.

## Objectives

- To learn four strategies to cope with strong resistance.
- To experience and practice these strategies.

**Group Size:** any
**Time Required:** 50 minutes

## Materials

- One copy of the Four Ways to "Get Your Foot in the Door" handout for each participant

# *Activity Flow*

1. Explain that, for most of us, the idea of being open to resistance is akin to welcoming a head cold. But it is one of life's paradoxes that the times when we are most eager to push our own causes are the very times we must be the most receptive to the resistance we are receiving. For example, salespeople try to avoid a resounding no from their customers. They do what they can to keep the sales opportunity alive. As the expression goes, they try to "get their foot in the door" rather then "have the door slammed in their face."

2. Distribute the Four Ways to "Get Your Foot in the Door" handout. Give participants a chance to read it over. Then discuss each suggestion from the handout.

3. As you present each strategy, ask participants to share examples in which each of the four strategies might apply.

4. Have participants form pairs. Have them discuss and apply as many of these strategies as they can to a situation of their choosing. Then ask them to develop a short skit that shows the use of one of these strategies. As pairs volunteer to conduct their skits, push for skits that cover all of the strategies.

5. Debrief the activity by asking participants, "What are you taking away from this activity?"

# Other Options

1. Ask participants to create their own ideas on ways "to get your foot in the door."

2. Have participants share stories of when these strategies helped them to be less resistant to someone else's advice.

# *Four Ways to "Get Your Foot in the Door"*

1. *Ask the resistor to merely listen to you.* Share your suggestion without expecting a response.

   Your example:

2. *Give the resistor useful information to read or watch* that provides relevant reasons a person might give your proposal a second look. Don't push the matter any further.

   Your example:

3. *Suggest a one-time experiment.* Ask the person to try something only once. Let the person control the "experiment."

   Your example:

4. *Urge the person to consider only one part* of your recommendation rather than the whole enchilada.

   Your example:

# 5 CONFLICT AND NEGOTIATION ⸻

# 20  Views of Conflict: A Word Association Game

## Introductory Remarks

I once read a book titled *Conflict for Cowards*. Most of us can identify with the title because conflict is often viewed as something to avoid rather than invite. This simple word-association game is a powerful way to reveal our negative views of conflict and can open up a discussion about the positive side of conflict.

## Objectives

- To show how our negativity toward conflict lessens opportunities for change.
- To consider how to change the way we perceive conflict.

**Group Size:** any

**Time Required:** 20 minutes

## Materials

- One copy of the Word Association handout for each participant
- Flip chart or whiteboard and markers

## Activity Flow

1. Ask participants to complete the Word Association handout. Give them 1 minute.

2. Invite participants to call out some of their associations. Record their words on a flip chart or whiteboard. Stop after 10 words.

3. Note that most or all the words are negative. [Common negative associations are *fighting, battle, unpleasant, nasty,* and so forth.] This suggests that we bring a negative attitude to most conflict situations.

4. Share that we don't have many positive words to describe conflict, yet conflict is a natural, normal, and necessary aspect of life. Point out that as long as there are differences among people, there will be conflicts and competing interests. Yet conflicts can create an opportunity to get things resolved that have been brewing under the surface. Conflicts can lead to new ideas. Conflicts can bring people closer together.

5. Offer the analogy that conflict, at best, is like an oyster struggling with a grain of sand to produce a pearl.

6. Debrief the activity by asking participants some of the following questions:

   - What positive words come to mind when you see the word *conflict?*

   - When has a conflict led to something better for you?

   - What are some inner thoughts on which you can focus to be open to conflict rather than resist it?

# Other Options ————————————————

1. Invite participants to suggest slogans that advertise a positive view of conflict. Examples might include:

   - Conflict brings opportunities for change.

   - Conflict is for leaders, not cowards.

   - Conflict is to be welcomed, not avoided.

2. Discuss the term "positive conflict." What can happen when groups and organizations create a positive conflict culture?

# *Word Association*

When you see the word CONFLICT, what words come to mind?

# 21 What You Bring to Conflict Situations: Experiencing Different Styles

## ─────Introductory Remarks─────

Through a variety of activities, participants experience feelings and behaviors they bring to conflict situations. The overall experience of participating in these activities may reveal things that are different from what participants expect. By obtaining a better fix on their styles, participants can more clearly evaluate their conflict styles and decide how and when they would like to try different styles.

## *Objectives*

- To clarify the strategies or styles for coping with conflict that each participant brings to an encounter.
- To experience different conflict styles.

**Group Size:** at least four

**Time Required:** 60 minutes

## *Materials*

- One copy of the Four Styles of Conflict handout for each participant
- Prepared slide or flip-chart page (see Step 8)

# *Activity Flow*

1. Ask participants to stand up and form a line. If they usually *"hate"* being in conflict situations, they should go to the head of the line. By contrast, if they typically *"relish"* conflict situations, they should find a place to the rear of the line. Participants who do not identify with either choice should find a place somewhere in the middle. Don't allow participants to bunch up in the middle. Urge them to create a single-file line. Use humor to help participants feel relaxed during the activity.

2. When the lineup is completed, ask participants to take chairs and sit in a semi-circle so that they can see each other while keeping their places. They should remain in the same order as the lineup.

3. Interview the two participants at each end of the semi-circle as to the feelings influencing their self-placement. Ask other participants to share their feelings about conflict. Note that discomfort with conflict is rather normal.

4. Use one or more game-like exercises that place participants in a conflict situation. Examples are:

   - Thumb wrestling in pairs

   - Debating someone (Find an issue that two partners truly disagree about, such as abortion, capital punishment, American foreign policy, etc.)

   - Breaking balloons (Have each participant blow up a balloon and tie it to her or his ankle with a string. Then give a signal to begin a game in which participants try to break one another's balloons by stepping on them. The last person to have an unbroken balloon is the winner.)

5. Debrief participants' feelings of aggression, defensiveness, defeat, and victory. Note strategies or styles for coping with conflict.

6. Distribute the Four Styles of Conflict handout and ask participants to read it. Explain that no one has a consistent conflict style. However, most people prefer one style to the other three. Ask for and respond to any

questions about the four style descriptions. Clarify that the two middle styles, persuasive and cooperative, are often confused. A persuasive person has few concerns about speaking up, even if other people are not happy with his or her position. A cooperative person is more selective about when to take a stand.

7. Inform participants that they will have the opportunity to use each of the four styles and compare their comfort levels with each. Divide participants into groups of four (if possible). Explain that each group will be asked to pretend they are on a team that has low morale and frequent tensions. Each member has a particular theory about what is wrong.

   - Person 1 believes that the team manager is not clear about priorities and should be asked to provide them.

   - Person 2 believes that team members need more social time together to get better acquainted on a personal level.

   - Person 3 believes that team members have different levels of commitment to the team's goals.

   - Person 4 believes that the team has a group of "personalities" that don't mix well and little can be done to turn things around.

8. Have each group count off 1 through 4 and assume the roles of Person 1, 2, 3, or 4. Before starting their discussions, display the following on newsprint or a slide.

| Person | 1 | 2 | 3 | 4 |
|--------|---|---|---|---|
| Round 1 | Confronting | Persuasive | Cooperative | Avoiding |
| Round 2 | Persuasive | Cooperative | Avoiding | Confronting |
| Round 3 | Cooperative | Avoiding | Confronting | Persuasive |
| Round 4 | Avoiding | Confronting | Persuasive | Cooperative |

9. Explain that the discussion will be interrupted every 5 minutes, thereby creating four "rounds." During each round, each team member will behave using the style assigned on the chart. Thus, over the 20-minute discussion, each member will adopt each one of the four styles (in a different order).

10. Suggest that participants act out their styles in subtle ways. It is generally not helpful to exaggerate any style.

11. When the four rounds are completed, invite each group to debrief the experience. You might use these questions:

   ■ Which style(s) were easy or hard for you to perform?

   ■ What feelings did you have from this experience about each style?

   ■ How could learning to use one of the styles that is new to you help you on the job?

# Other Options

1. There are several instruments that assess conflict style. Obtain one of these and request that your participants complete it. Such instruments usually contain suggestions to debrief the assessment.

2. Discuss how to respond to other people's styles, given one's own style. For example, what advice would one give to a person with a persuasive style to deal with a person with an avoiding style?

# *Four Styles of Conflict*

1. **Confronting** people tend to be aggressive, "in your face" types who can be bullying or judgmental.

2. **Persuasive** individuals are assertive and don't hesitate to stand up for themselves.

3. **Cooperative** types are comfortable doing more listening than talking. They are often willing to be conciliatory, but will speak up if an issue is important to them.

4. **Avoiding** people would prefer to cross the street rather than engage in a conflict. They may withdraw or accept situations they dislike, rather than speak up.

# The Ten-Thousand-Dollar Challenge: Working Through a Conflict

---
## Introductory Remarks

This role-playing exercise is designed to demonstrate how two people can work through a conflict and possibly achieve a win-win resolution. I like this activity because it involves the entire group as two people enact a conflict.

---

## Objectives

- To show the difference between *positions* (what you want) and *interests* (the underlying concerns behind the positions).

- To practice using questions to help resolve a conflict.

**Group Size:** any

**Time Required:** 20 minutes

## Materials

- One copy of the Questions for Understanding Interests handout for each participant

## Activity Flow

1. Recruit (ahead of time) a volunteer to assist you in role playing a conflict between two people who have been jointly awarded $10,000. Explain that the volunteer and you work together as consultants. The prize was given to you because of your outstanding contribution toward building cohesion in a diverse community.

2. Assign the position each party will take: You want to give the money to a charity or other worthy cause, while the volunteer wants to spend it on travel. Make sure the volunteer understands that the two of you will alternate playing out your conflict, allowing the participants to ask questions to uncover more information about your needs. Although the two of you will start out diametrically opposed, you should both begin to show more interest and empathy toward the other's positions as the participants are successful in uncovering your needs.

3. Explain to participants the following conditions: you and the volunteer are business partners who have been awarded the $10,000 prize. You must spend the money (you cannot invest it) and you can't divide it (and so must agree on how to spend it together).

4. Instruct the group that their job is to serve as consultants to the two of you by asking you questions to uncover your underlying interests. (By now, they will already know each other's stated positions.) Forbid them to offer solutions!

5. Distribute the Questions for Understanding Interests handout as a "crib sheet" for the participants.

6. Role play the conflict for a few minutes, then stop the action. Don't allow anyone to get into any solutions. Have fun, with both parties being initially adamant about their positions.

7. Instruct participants to ask you each questions to elicit your interests (such as what you hope to obtain from your position). *Do not allow any questions that suggest solutions to the conflict.*

8. Continue the role play until a point is reached at which each side has a better understanding of the other.

9. Ask participants what has been accomplished with the information the two parties have stated publicly.

10. Suggest, if not stated by participants, that two things are accomplished:

   ▪ Each side understands the other better and will be more motivated to seek a win-win solution, if possible.

   ▪ The new information may hint at an actual resolution to the conflict.

11. Now ask participants to suggest possible win-win solutions to the conflict. (For example, a travel destination can include a charitable act or the tax deduction for a charitable contribution of $10,000 can be given to the person who wants some money for travel or another luxury.)

# Other Options

1. Invite participants to suggest slogans that advertise a positive view of conflict. Examples might include:

   - Conflict brings opportunities for change.

   - Conflict is for leaders, not cowards.

   - Conflict is to be welcomed, not avoided.

2. Discuss the benefit of working toward a win-win solution, even if one is never reached. Perhaps, the two parties can reach a resolution when they have the same goal but prefer a different way to obtain it. However, if value differences underlie the conflict, it is very difficult to reach a resolution or even a compromise.

# *Questions for Understanding Interests*

1. What do you want? Why?

2. How did you come to that decision?

3. How do you feel about your partner's preference?

4. What concerns you about your partner's preference?

5. What do you want your partner to understand about your position?

6. What would you do if you were in your partner's shoes?

7. Are you open to an entirely different solution from what either of you wants?

8. What else matters to you in this situation?

# 23 Role Reversal: Arguing the Flip Side

┌─────────────**Introductory Remarks**─────────────┐

This exercise allows participants to experience reversing roles, a time-honored conflict-resolution technique. One effective way to defuse a conflict situation so severe that it is blocking action is to have the participants reverse roles. People may have boxed themselves into all-or-nothing thinking patterns and may not know how to escape from that trap. As they concentrate on presenting each other's viewpoints, it is possible the participants can resolve misunderstandings, place their perceptions on a more realistic level, and reach a clearer understanding of each other's positions.

└─────────────────────────────────────────────────┘

## *Objectives*

- To learn and practice role reversal.
- To uncover insights about the value of putting yourself in someone else's shoes.

**Group Size:** any

**Time Required:** 30 to 40 minutes

**Materials:** none

## *Activity Flow*

1. Identify an issue in which participants have boxed themselves into all-or-nothing thinking patterns. Present the following scenario (or another of your choosing):

   "Consider, for example, a high-rise condominium association where there is a dispute about whether to allow members to put up for rent any apartment they own. The association is split between those in favor and those opposed. You will want each side to consider the other's point of view."

   Create two groups. Group A supports the right to rent. Group B does not. Allow for 10 minutes of debate between the two sides.

2. Now ask participants to be willing to experience a different way of discussing. Explain that you will ask the group to spend from 10 to 20 minutes discussing the dispute that has arisen. During that time, participants will be asked to take on the position of their previous opponent. As a result, those in favor previously will now be opposed.

3. Facilitate the role-reversal discussion. Keep encouraging participants to stay in role. While there may be some laughter during this process, try to keep the mood serious.

4. After the time is up, ask each side these questions:

   - Did you feel that your own views were accurately stated by others adopting your position?

   - What insights did you obtain from arguing the flip side?

5. Now continue a normal discussion of the conflict to determine whether the role-reversal process has helped to move the group beyond where it was.

## Other Options

1. Pair up participants with opposite views and ask them to argue the flip sides with each other. This may be less awkward than conducting a whole-group discussion.

2.  If the group is a small one and the members know each other relatively well, it's fun to switch identities instead of just positions. Simply have the participants move their name tags and pretend to be the other person while presenting the other person's position.

3.  As an alternative to this role-reversal exercise, list competing ideas in the group. Ask participants to state the advantages of ideas that differ from their own. Publicly stating the good point of an opponent's solution may reduce the tension in a polarized group.

# 24 Rating Methods to Deal with Conflict: Yours and Theirs

## Introductory Remarks

At first, this activity appears to be a simple survey of methods used to deal with conflict. The surprise arises when participants are asked to respond to each item from two perspectives—their own and the perspective of another. Invariably, participants rate themselves more positively than they rate others.

## Objectives

- To discover that people are more negative about the actions of others than they are about their own.
- To assess the impact of this bias in conflict situations.

**Group Size:** any

**Time Required:** 15 to 30 minutes (depending on the number of participants)

## Materials

- Flip chart and markers
- One copy of the Fourteen Methods for Dealing with Conflict handout for each participant

## Activity Flow

1. Divide participants into small groups of three or four members. Ask them to share with each other *"the most prevalent reasons that conflict occurs"* in

their own lives at home and/or at work (decide which context is appropriate to your training group). Use one frequent reason as an example (such as " misunderstanding").

2. Ask each group to pick typical reasons to share with the full group.

3. Obtain and list one contribution at a time from each group until you have filled a newsprint sheet.

4. Distribute the Fourteen Methods handout and ask participants to circle the five methods they personally use most often to deal with conflict. Urge them to be truthful.

5. Now ask them to put a square around the five methods used most often by other people in their personal and/or professional lives. (A single item may be circled *and* squared.)

6. Tabulate across the full group the votes for each method circled and "squared." Observe whether there are any significant discrepancies. Quite likely, participants will see themselves as using "positive" methods (Items 9, 11, 13, and 14) more often than they perceive others using them. If this is the case, ask participants to explain the discrepancy between how people see themselves versus how they see others.

7. Point out, if not already said, the human tendency to view oneself more favorably than the way we view others. Ask participants to comment on how this tendency affects people's behavior in conflict situations.

# Other Options

1. Further explore the power of projection. Discuss why people view themselves more favorably than they view others. Ask for examples beyond interpersonal relationships.

2. Ask participants to give out the Fourteen Methods handout to others at work, requesting that they identify methods they and others use to deal with conflict. Note whether positive methods are more often chosen than negative methods.

# *Fourteen Methods for Dealing with Conflict*

1.  Be indirect; only hint at the problem bothering you.

2.  Find someone other than yourself on whom to blame the situation.

3.  Use sarcasm in talking about the situations of others.

4.  Seek a specific scapegoat.

5.  Make an active effort to smooth over the tension or to live with the situation, even if it may be negative.

6.  Blow up; let off steam.

7.  Hide your feelings at the moment and only reveal them later to friends in private.

8.  Put your energy into other unrelated activities or interests.

9.  Spend time listening and gathering additional information.

10. Back down under pressure.

11. Find common ground.

12. Complain to others.

13. Make an effort to seek creative solutions.

14. Seek clarification and more information about the situation.

# 25 Breaking a Stalemate: Steps to Move Forward

## ─── Introductory Remarks ───

In this role-play exercise, participants experience a
conflict that reaches a stalemate. After a debriefing of
the stalemated conflict, they are introduced to a four-step
model to move forward.

## *Objectives*

- To experience a stalemated conflict.

- To learn and practice a four-step process that could break a stalemate.

**Group Size:** any

**Time Required:** 30 minutes

## *Materials*

- One copy of the Four Steps for Breaking a Stalemate handout for each participant

## *Activity Flow*

1. Divide the entire group into subgroups of four to six members. Within the subgroups, ask participants to count off A, B, A, B, and so on. If there is an odd number, there will be an extra A person.

2. Give these directions:

"The A's are to role play people who feel strongly that profanity should not be allowed universally on television, even if there are parental locks available or any other method to create self-selected controls. Develop at least three objections to the use of profanity on TV. Assume that your position has no exceptions or compromise.

"The B's are to role play people who feel strongly that profanity should be allowed universally on television. Assume that parental locks are available or any other method to create self-selected controls. Develop at least three objections to the prohibition of profanity on TV. Assume that your position has no exceptions or compromise."

3. Provide a few minutes for each subgroup (A's and B's) to prepare their arguments.

4. Ask A's and B's in each subgroup to press their best arguments and to rebut the opponent's arguments as strongly as they can. Request that no offers to compromise be made in order to create an eventual stalemate. Allow from 5 to 10 minutes for the debate.

5. Distribute the Four Steps to Breaking a Stalemate handout and go over the methods.

6. Ask each side to prepare a four-part presentation that includes the four elements of breaking a stalemate:

7. Invite each side to make its presentation in each subgroup.

8. Ask each side to comment on the other's presentation.

   ▪ How understanding was the other side?

   ▪ What suggestions did they offer that hold promise?

9. Reconvene the entire group and obtain feedback about the usefulness of the four steps. Indicate that the exchange may not lead to a resolution, but at least the quality of discussion will be raised so that ongoing dialogue is possible.

10. Inquire whether any ideas that emerged could form the basis for moving to a win-win resolution of the problem.

# Other Options ——————————————————————

1. Use any of the following conflicts in lieu of the one provided or create one of your own:

   - Healthcare reform

   - Tax reform

   - Layoffs of 15 percent of the workforce to avoid bankruptcy

   - Abolition of employee performance appraisals

2. Briefly present the well-known ideas in *Getting to Yes* by Ury and Fisher. Make special mention of the difference between "positions" and "interests." Break participants into subgroups of four to six participants and ask each group to create a skit in which a conflict is resolved by focusing on needs rather than on positions.

# Four Steps for Breaking a Stalemate

## The Conflict We're Having

Discuss and agree on the positions being taken that oppose each other. Be objective and descriptive and show that you have listened well to your opponents. Don't disparage their positions. Be respectful.

For example, consider a conflict between the academic dean of a college and the faculty on grade inflation. The faculty might state: *"It seems that we have opposite views about grade inflation. You want a greater distribution of grades so that we appear to have higher standards than what is reflected in the current grade distribution. We think that the higher grades reflect well on us as a faculty. We must be doing something right."*

## What Concerns Us

Ask each party to share underlying feelings, concerns, and needs about the issue in conflict.

The faculty might further say: *"We are concerned that students will become obsessed with how they are graded rather than how they can be effective learners. We also worry that focusing on grade inflation emphasizes making things tougher for students, not rethinking what our basic teaching goals are and what we can do to facilitate them."*

## What We'd Like to Suggest

Each party shares a creative suggestion to get beyond where the group is stuck.

The faculty might then say: *"What would be ideal is to agree to be more explicit about the performance criteria for different grading outcomes. If most students do well, there's no reason to have a grading curve."*

## What We're Willing to Do About It

Each party makes a statement about the actions it is prepared to take to create a better situation.

The faculty then concludes: *"We'd be willing to submit to the academic dean our current grading criteria and obtain his recommendations on how they can be made more clear."*

# 6 CREATIVITY AND PROBLEM SOLVING —

**Getting Ready for Brainstorming: Creative Warm-Ups**

> ───────── **Introductory Remarks** ─────────
>
> A group's creativity is fostered by thinking "outside the box"—looking at issues in new ways and developing novel solutions to problems. To go beyond the same tried-and-true ideas, it is helpful to warm up participants before launching into the real business of the group. There are a number of ways to help the brain become limber and ready for serious creative problem solving.

## *Objectives*

- To experience fun, quick brainstorming.
- To assess the value of warming up before tackling serious brainstorming.

**Group Size:** any

**Time Required:** 10 minutes or less

## *Materials*

- (Optional) One copy of the Nine-Dot Problem for each participant
- (Optional) One copy of the Nine-Dot Problem Solution handout for each participant

## *Activity Flow*

1. Tell participants that you thought it might be a fun to have a short warm-up before doing some serious creative problem solving.

2. Select one or more of the following warm-up activities:

   Think of as many *uses* (even crazy ones) as you can for any of the following:

   | | |
   |---|---|
   | ruler | sticky note |
   | hat | necktie |
   | brick | pencil |
   | sponge | an aluminum can |

   [Of course, the possible objects are endless. Do some of your own brainstorming.]

   Think of *novel ways* to do things such as:

   | | |
   |---|---|
   | peeling a navel orange | simplifying your life |
   | holding a meeting | greeting someone "hello" |
   | traveling from coast to coast | |

   Think of as many *similes* as you can, such as:

   - *A meeting is like a . . .*
   - *Our organization is like a . . .*
   - *This project is like a . . .*
   - *A facilitator is like a . . .*

   Think of as many excuses as you can for:

   - *Being late to a meeting*
   - *Wearing socks that don't match*
   - *Running out of gas*
   - *A "bounced" check*

Think of as many names/titles as you can for:

- *A book on effective meetings*

- *A film about Barack Obama*

- *A bowling team*

- *A cemetery*

Think of as many thought experiments as you can, such as:

- *What might happen if no men attended this meeting?*

- *What might happen if dogs could speak?*

- *What might happen if everyone in the world prayed sometime today?*

- *What might happen if most people had to work the night shift?*

- *What might happen if computers were banned?*

- *What might happen if there were snow on the ground year-round where you live?*

3. Debrief the warm-up(s). How would one or more brief warm-ups help them to tackle serious, real-world situations that require new thinking?

# Other Options

1. Do warm-up activities that are nonverbal, such as creative doodling or imitating musical instruments.

2. Give participants "the nine-dot problem," the classic exercise that created the expression "thinking outside the box." (The solution requires extending the lines beyond the confines of the nine dots, which give the visual impression of a box.)

# Nine-Dot Problem

*Instructions:* Connect all nine dots with no more than four straight lines. Do not lift your pencil off the paper. You will have five minutes to find the solution.

# Nine-Dot Problem Solution

*Note to facilitator:* Do NOT photocopy this solution with the problem

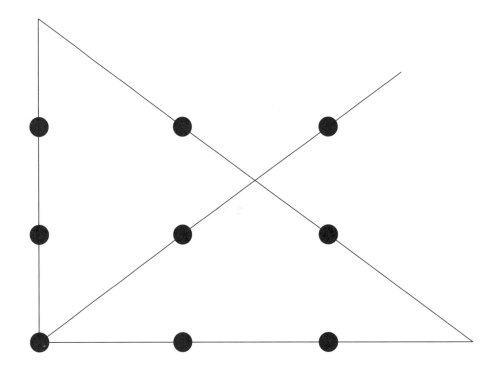

#  Part Changing: Demonstrating a Technique to Increase Creativity

## Introductory Remarks

Often, brainstorming new ideas is difficult because the size of the problem taxes the creative imagination of the group. One way to overcome this situation is to break the problem, issue, or goal down into its constituent parts and examine each part separately. Then participants can brainstorm ideas involving each part. Doing this will help to loosen up participants, and they may produce some truly novel and productive ideas. I have been amazed by the impact of this tool. Individuals and groups who feel they have exhausted their creative capacity are impressed by how it unleashes new creative ideas.

## *Objectives*

- To introduce a tool to enhance idea generation.
- To experience the tool and assess the results.

**Group Size:** any

**Time Required:** 10 to 30 minutes

**Materials:** none

# *Activity Flow*

1. State a problem, issue, or goal about which you want to have a brainstorming session (for example, how to improve the way a president is elected in the United States).

2. Next, ask the participants to think about all the elements or parts of the problem, issue, or goal *by breaking it down*. As an example, consider the planning of a successful fundraising race. These are some aspects of the project to be considered:

   - A slogan

   - The course to be run

   - A length for the race

   - A date for the race (Is Saturday better than Sunday? Rain date or no? Maybe a holiday weekend?)

   - Prizes

   - A deadline for entries

   - Emergency services

   - Publicity—before, at, and after the race.

3. Explain that once the event has been separated in to different parts, it is a lot easier to unleash creative ideas. To demonstrate this, use the example of electing a U.S. president. Ask participants to suggest current elements of the election process. They might include:

   - *Campaigning*

   - *Candidate qualifications*

   - *The voting process: how and when*

   - *The primary system*

   - *Determining the winner (electoral versus popular vote)*

4. Create groups of four to six participants. Ask each group to look over these elements and brainstorm changes, such as letting people vote online.

5. Ask each group to post its ideas.

6. Debrief the experience:

   - Assess how well the process worked.

   - Identify workplace situations in which part-changing would be helpful (for example, improving customer service in a retail store).

# Other Options

1. Warm up the group by giving them one or two common items and asking them to generate its parts or elements. Here are some examples:

   - A bathtub (shape, color, size, etc.)

   - A belt (length, number of holes, material, etc.)

   - A party (invitation, theme, activities, cost)

2. Have participants brainstorm things that have improved a lot by changing just a few parts. Here are some examples:

   - Putting products and services online (books, banking)

   - Using colors other than white (appliances, tennis balls, sheets)

   - Altering size (computers, refrigerators, cameras)

#  Brainwriting: An Alternative to Generating Ideas Verbally

## Introductory Remarks

Brainwriting is a quick and efficient way to draw out the best ideas from a group, and it levels the playing field in several ways. I have found it to be a refreshing change from verbally generating ideas. Brainwriting provides equal weight for each idea, whether it's suggested by the CEO or by the janitor. In addition, it provides equal play for both extroverts and introverts. Because the exercise is a written one, those who don't ordinarily speak up often express themselves more freely. It also prevents ideas from being blocked, and perhaps lost, by those more articulate participants who tend to dominate with the spoken word.

## Objectives

- To experience the brainwriting process.
- To identify the features and benefits of brainwriting.

**Group Size:** six to eight.
**Time Required:** 20 to 30 minutes

## Materials

- Blank sheets of paper and a pen or pencil for each participant
- (Optional) Flip chart and markers for each subgroup

# *Activity Flow*

1. Indicate that brainstorming can be a written as well as a verbal process.

2. Create groups of six to eight participants. Explain that you want everyone to pretend that he or she works for a start-up team-building company that provides training and consultation. The yet-unnamed company wants to create an attractive name. Pass out blank sheets of paper and pens or pencils and ask each person to write on the paper one potential name.

3. Encourage participants to let their thoughts run free and remind them that no idea is too silly to write down. Another person may see a practical side to that idea, and it may be turned into something not so silly after all.

4. In each subgroup, participants should pass their papers to the persons on their right.

5. Ask each participant to read the idea and either try to build on that idea or use it to come up with an entirely new thought. Tell the participants to write their ideas just beneath the original idea and again pass the paper to the person to the right. Continue in the same way until each paper has a list of six to eight ideas.

6. Have participants pass the sheets back to the first writer so he or she can see how others have built on the original idea.

7. Ask the person who wrote his or her idea first to choose one or two of the best ideas from the sheet and then discuss them with the group.

8. Debrief the experience by asking participants to share their reactions to the process and identify situations in which brainwriting might be a useful alternative.

# Other Options

1. Have participants practice brainwriting more than once to develop their skills.

2. Have each group choose the best name from the initial brainwriting process. Ask the group to place the name on the top of a flip chart. Have groups circulate among the flip-chart entries and write any further ideas.

## **29** Inspired Cut-Outs: Freeing the Mind

---**Introductory Remarks**---

Collages, those wonderful kaleidoscopic creations of bits and pieces of paper that form pictures or just patterns, can provide real inspiration for problem solving. Your participants can freshen their approach to a solution and be more creative by leafing through colorful magazines. When their eyes catch certain pictures, it may change the direction of their thoughts, turning them slightly so they see a different view, or it even may force a quick change of course. This creative exercise may help participants to see a problem they're working on in a slightly different light. Paging through a magazine frees the mind even as the person concentrates on something else.

## *Objectives*

- To demonstrate the power of right-brain thinking.
- To gain skill in using visual ideas to solve practical problems.

**Group Size:** up to twenty-four participants
**Time Required:** 20 to 30 minutes

## *Materials*

- **A** large assortment of magazines with colorful pictures, scissors, paste, and blank paper for each subgroup

# *Activity Flow*

1. Create groups of four to six participants. Distribute a large assortment of magazines with colorful pictures, scissors, paste, and blank paper to each group. Give each group a different problem to solve. Examples include:

   ■ How to make meetings more effective

   ■ How to reduce costs in their business

   ■ How to manage stress

   ■ How to motivate employees to higher performance

   Explain the concept behind the activity—seeking new ideas for solving their assigned problem using visual materials.

2. Tell the participants they may search in the magazines for pieces to make a collage—an abstract composition made with fragments of paper.

3. They may, if they wish, actually cut up the magazine and paste together a collage, but they don't have to go that far. Participants can form a mental collage by seeking out ideas and themes that are attractive to them.

   ■ *For example, a group of architects might be frustrated by the necessity of fitting manufacturing equipment into a certain plan. As they let their minds wander through picture pages, building either mental or real collages, they're more likely to be receptive to a new idea, a change of design, or to see something in a pattern that sparks their imaginations.*

   ■ *A group of business strategists stumped in their attempt to move from a hierarchical system to a flatter organization might see a picture of a flock of geese that may help them visualize the company's proposed structure more easily.*

   ■ *At a meeting, a voluntary group was discussing how to recruit new volunteers and felt stuck. Looking at an image of wind surfers found in a TV ad, someone said: "We're not making volunteering sound like it's fun or cool. Why don't we think of ways to promote volunteering by appealing to the fun people will have rather than the 'contribution' they would be making to society?"*

4. Allow at least 15 minutes for groups to create their collages. Then give them additional time to look at what they created and identify ideas that would help solve their assigned problem.

5. Have each group present what the members did.

6. Debrief the experience, focusing on the value of using a right-brain process to look at problems in unique ways. For example:

   ■ It frees the mind of assumptions that limit problem solving.

   ■ It often leads to new ideas.

   ■ The ideas can be interesting, even if they are not logical or immediately sensible.

# Other Options

1. Display a variety of both abstract and realistic photos/graphics and challenge participants to envision practical ideas to address any of the problems posed above.

2. Discuss the Herrmann Brain Dominance Instrument (HBDI), a system claimed to measure and describe thinking preferences in people, developed by William "Ned" Herrmann.

# 30 Wearing Someone Else's Shoes: Taking a Different Perspective

## Introductory Remarks

Here is an idea to bring some creativity and fun to any meeting. Participants are asked to assume the identity of someone else in order to loosen their own thinking about an issue facing the group. What I like about this activity is how it requires participants to look at an issue, task, or problem from different perspectives.

## *Objectives*

- To experience another person's perspective.
- To apply perspective taking to real-world problems.

**Group Size:** any

**Time Required:** 10 to 30 minutes

## *Materials*

- Index cards with assigned roles/identities (see Step 3)

## *Activity Flow*

1. Explain to participants that we often look at an issue from our own frames of reference. Sometimes, taking someone else's perspective casts a new light on things.

2. Ask participants to assume that they work in any of the following settings and are grappling with the development of ideas for improvement:

   - A company that provides educational literature about reducing carbon emissions

- A shelter for homeless people

- A bank that wants to assist people who do not currently have bank accounts

- A wedding planning service

3. Give out cards to participants with the identity of someone else. (Depending on the group size, each participant can receive a different identity or two or more can share the same identity.)

    You might use categories that are relevant to the situation:

    | | |
    |---|---|
    | customer | board member |
    | community member | top management |
    | student | consultant |
    | volunteer | competitor |
    | parent | police officer |

    Or ask participants to switch to a person of a different:

    | | |
    |---|---|
    | gender | age group |
    | geographic location | personality type |
    | ethnic, religious, or racial background | |

    Or you might choose well-known people. Here are some suggestions:

    | | |
    |---|---|
    | Bill Gates | Martin Luther King, Jr. |
    | Michelle Obama | Chris Rock |
    | Moses | Oprah Winfrey |
    | Mother Theresa | Stephen Covey |
    | John Lennon | Jane Austen |

Or, if the participants are well-known to each other, assign each participant the identity of someone else in the group.

4. Provide some way for each participant to show his or her identity. Ask each participant to think about how the ideas under consideration might look to the person whose identity is being assumed.

5. Request that participants discuss the issue "wearing someone else's shoes." Encourage them to really take on the identity of the person assigned to them. Continue the discussion for as long as it seems useful. Even 5 minutes might be enough time to shake participants from their own frames of reference and enable them to view things differently.

6. Debrief the experience. Ask participants what they were feeling during the activity and how it affected what they said or did not say.

# Other Options

1. Consider providing costume items such as a hat, a sign, a pipe, a crown, and so forth to dramatize the process.

2. Create an imagined community meeting that is called to reduce crime. What would different kinds of people say at that meeting?

# 31 Making Decisions After Brainstorming: Narrowing the Options

## Introductory Comments

Most people know how to brainstorm in groups but don't know ways to reach a decision afterward. They fail to establish evaluation criteria appropriate to the situation. These factors help to rule in or rule out ideas. For example, an idea may be difficult to implement. In this activity, participants develop criteria to narrow down a brainstormed list of ideas.

## *Objectives*

- To recognize that brainstorming requires a decision-making process to narrow the options.

- To experience the use of criteria to narrow down a brainstormed list of ideas.

**Group Size:** any

**Time Required:** 30 minutes

**Materials:** none

## *Activity Flow*

1.  Explain that brainstorming is not only a way to increase creativity but also an excellent process to prevent endless discussion and debate. By

allowing several ideas to be contributed without criticism, brainstorming promotes a group rather than an individual mindset.

2. Indicate that brainstorming, however, presents its own problems. Once a group generates a number of ideas, it can still get bogged down in deciding which ones are the best.

3. Form teams of four to eight members and ask each team to quickly brainstorm and record uses that could be made of a "belt" by people marooned on an island. After 3 minutes, stop the teams and ask them to choose their two most original ideas. Have them share these with the other groups.

4. Point out that these decisions were not especially difficult because the task was frivolous and nothing was at stake.

5. Now provide the teams with a more challenging, real-life brainstorming task (for example, how can performance reviews be improved?). Guide them through the process in these steps:

   ■ Generate at least five ideas or solutions

   ■ Seek clarification of people's suggestions but do not express disagreement or reservations

   ■ Next, generate criteria to evaluate the available ideas or solutions (cost, time factors, etc.)

   ■ Evaluate each idea/solution, one at a time.

   ■ Discuss and decide which two ideas have the highest priority

6. Reconvene the entire group. Debrief the exercise. What worked well? What did not work well? Would you use this process with other people in your workplace? How? Where?

# Other Options

1. Explain that brainstorming ensures that everyone has equal input, but other procedures are still needed to efficiently get a group reading on issues. Describe and refer to the example of "multi-voting" (voting to

select the most favored ideas). In this procedure, a first vote is taken to identify the top half of those ideas. The bottom half is then eliminated. Open discussion follows to assess the remaining ideas. A second vote is taken so that half of the remaining ideas stay on the list. Again, a discussion ensues of the remaining ideas, followed by a third vote. The process of voting and discussion continues until one idea remains. Walk through "multi-voting" after an initial list of ten to fifteen endearing names are brainstormed (such as honey, sweetheart, love, dude).

2. Practice narrowing down a brainstormed list of "negative ideas" such as the worst Valentine gifts.

# 7 DIVERSITY

# 32 Being in the Minority: Simulating an Everyday Reality

---
## Introductory Remarks

In this exercise, participants are asked to form groups in which many will be in the majority while some will be in the minority. This is an experiential activity for which the debriefing is demanding. The facilitator's challenge is to encourage open, honest conversation about the impact of being in the minority. Your judgment about how the activity is unfolding is critical. You need to "read" the sensitivities in the group and decide how to bring out those disclosures participants are willing to provide.

---

## *Objectives*

- To experience being excluded.
- To identify feelings of pride, indifference, and marginalization in different groups.
- To achieve a better understanding of people different from you.

**Group Size:** at least ten participants

**Time Required:** 45 minutes

## *Materials*

- Flip chart or whiteboard and markers

# *Activity Flow*

1. Ask the group to give examples of "minority" groups. Especially encourage them to share "minority" groups they actually belong to. Record the groups mentioned on a flip chart or whiteboard. (Depending on the openness of your participants, some examples might be more personally disclosing than others.)

2. Tell the participants the following:

   "I'm going to call out several 'minority' groups. I have my own list, but I might also use some of the examples you have already mentioned that I just recorded. When you hear mention of a minority group to which you belong, get up from your seats and go to the back of the room. When you are not a member of that group, wait until the minority group assembles and then go to the front of the room. When you reach your designated place, I will give you further instructions."

3. Create (or modify) a list from the choices below. Choose five or six from those you predict will match your group's composition and best contribute to the objectives of this exercise. (*Warning:* some are fairly benign and some are fairly sensitive.)

   ■ People with blue eyes

   ■ People who are left-handed

   ■ People who can not touch their toes from an erect, standing position.

   ■ People who are non-Christians (Jews, Muslims, Hindi, Buddhist, etc.)

   ■ People who are single

   ■ People over fifty (or under twenty-five)

   ■ People who cannot swim

   ■ People who do not believe in God

   ■ People who are gay or lesbian

   ■ People who are not Caucasian

4. With each category, give participants a chance to assemble in the front or back of the room. When there, ask the "minority" group members to share their feelings about being in the minority with each other. Encourage them to relate times in their lives that were sources of pride and tension. Ask the "majority" group members to share their feelings of pride and tension. (If the number of people is large, have them meet in smaller groupings.)

5. Next, have a "group-to-group" exchange, using the questions below as a guide to opening up honest communication. You can set up this exchange in many ways. Choose the way that best fits the time you have available, the size of the total group, and space for people to stand or sit and discuss.

   Questions for the group-to-group exchange:

   - What happened during this exercise? How were you feeling as it progressed?

   - How did you feel when you were part of the minority?

   - What are some experiences you might have shared with people similar to you?

   - How has this exercise heightened your awareness about people different from you?

6. Do a final debriefing with the total group. Ask: "What are you taking away from this activity?"

# Other Options

1. Request up to four volunteers who represent one of the minority groups listed in the directions above or new ones of your choosing. Explain that they are volunteering to be on a panel in front of their peers. Use some of the following questions or add your own. Also, solicit questions from the audience. Do not force a panelist to answer a question not to his or her liking. If you wish, let the person say: "I'll take a pass on that one . . . with dignity."

- Have you felt in your lifetime that you were a victim of discrimination? Marginalized (often referred to as the "other")? Teased? Just uncomfortable in the presence of others not like you?

- What positive feelings about your minority group do you have? Any negative feelings?

- What suggestions to you have for others about how they perceive and treat you?

2. Ask participants to close their eyes and visualize being a member of one of the following groups to which they do NOT belong in real life:

   - Gay or lesbian

   - Physically challenged

   - Financially "poor"

   - A citizen of a country other than the United States

   - A Jew or Muslim

Give participants some time to make their choices. Once they have done so, ask them to get into their "character" and imagine the rest of group staring at them . . . ignoring them . . . verbally humiliating them. Also ask them to think about perceptions that others would have of them but would keep to themselves. Use a format, such as pairs, small groups, fishbowl/panel, that allows them to share their experiences assuming minority identities.

# **33** I've Been Curious: Questions I Have Been Afraid to Ask

## Introductory Remarks

People who are different from us in a significant way can make us uncomfortable in their presence. The more contact, and certainly the more dialogue between groups, the more tensions are lessened. I first created a version of this activity many years ago for an inter-faith group. It was amazing to see the intimacy level rise within this group after we did this activity for the first few times we met. I have since used it in diversity training with similar results.

## *Objectives*

- To increase the level of intimacy in diverse groups.
- To learn the value of sharing and dialogue.

**Group Size:** any

**Time Required:** at least 30 minutes

## *Materials*

- Three index cards and a pen or pencil for each participant

## *Activity Flow*

1. Explain that many people are curious about others who are different from themselves, but are afraid to ask questions. For example, many

people are curious how a gay or lesbian person has been able to function in a marriage with a straight partner.

2. Have participants share some of the reasons why they're reluctant to ask questions. Included on the list may be any of the following:

   - It's not my business.

   - I'm afraid I will insult the other person.

   - I'm concerned that the other person will think I am naïve or clueless.

   - I don't want to appear insensitive or discriminatory.

3. Provide a diverse list of factors that create difference between people, such as:

   - gender

   - race

   - ethnicity

   - age

   - ability

   - religion

   - culture

   Add others that may be relevant to your participants.

4. Distribute three index cards per participant. Ask participants to write up to three questions, one per card. Each card can pertain to as many "groups" as the participant wants. Encourage them to mix "gutsy" and "soft" questions. Give these examples:

   - Why don't Jews believe that Jesus was the Son of God?

   - Why do Asians do well in school?

   - How did you, as an African-American, feel when Obama was elected president?

5. Collect all the cards and shuffle them. Beginning with the top of the deck of cards, read the question on each card and ask for volunteer(s) to respond. Go through as many cards as possible in the time available.

If the process is taking too long, end by merely reading each card so that the group hears all the questions.

6. Debrief the experience with these questions:

   ■ Was it worthwhile?

   ■ Did you think that the questions were useful overall?

   ■ Did you think that the group's responses were useful overall? In what way?

# Other Options

1. Use the same exercise but conduct it in smaller groups to facilitate more exchange.

2. Create a rotating panel discussion. Obtain one to three representatives from each "group" and have them serve as a panel to field questions about themselves. Create more panels as time permits.

# 34 Setting the Record Straight: Things About Me and Others Like Me

## Introductory Remarks

This activity is the flip side of "I've Been Curious: Questions I Have Been Afraid to Ask." Here, participants have the opportunity to state things about a group to which they belong. It's less risky than "I've Been Curious" and also serves the purpose of finding out more about others not like you.

## Objectives

- To have the opportunity to express positive statements about a group to which you belong.

- To gain an appreciation of different groups.

**Group Size:** at least six

**Time Required:** 20 minutes

## Materials

- One copy of the Sentence Completions handout for each participant

- An index card for each participant

## Activity Flow

1. Distribute the Sentence Completions handout and an index card to each participant. Ask participants to complete the incomplete sentences. They

should be things they believe to be true and that they are proud of. (For example, a gay man wrote, "One thing I would like others to know about gay men is that we are often devoted fathers.")

2. Ask participants to share and explain their endings with partners.

3. Next, ask each participant to write down ONE of his or her completed sentences on an index card. Have the cards passed around a group so that each participant can read what others have written. (There is no need to indicate the author of the card.) If there are more than fifteen participants, have the cards passed around in two groups rather than one. All cards should be passed clockwise. If they are passed in the order in which they were received, every participant will have read all the cards when his or her card comes back to him or her.

4. When the process is completed, debrief the experience. Use some of these questions:

   - Did some cards surprise you?

   - Which cards would you like the author to explain further?

   - Did you like the experience of sharing your sentiments with each other?

# Other Options

1. Use a call-on-the-next-speaker format so that anyone who would like to share one of his or her completions with the entire group may do so.

2. Conduct the sharing using a go-around. Each person shares one of his or her cards with the entire group, adding whatever else he or she would like to say. (Any participant has the right to "pass.") Discuss any questions that a particular card raises.

# *Sentence Completions*

From the list below, circle "groups" to which you belong:

- Male
- Female
- Christian
- Jewish
- Muslim
- White
- Black
- Single parent
- Homosexual
- Physically challenged
- Nerd/Geek
- Boomer Generation
- Hispanic
- Asian
- Add others:

Select one or more of the groups you have circled and complete the following incomplete sentence for each one:

- One thing I would like others to know about [selected group] is that we. . . .

# 35  Unlocking Memories: Self-Disclosures in a Diverse Group

## Introductory Remarks

This exercise is both high-risk and high-gain. Re-encountering what you have previously experienced can be painful, even traumatic—or it can be liberating. Moreover, doing this with a diverse group of people can be scary or revealing. I like activities with high self-disclosure precisely because they bring together an otherwise disparate group of participants.

## Objectives

- To show how a diverse group of people have much in common.
- To understand that mutual understanding involves risk and hard work.

**Group Size:** any
**Time Required:** 45 minutes
**Materials:** none

## Activity Flow

1. Explain to participants that you will be conducting a mental-imagery activity to connect participants with personal images and memories about diversity and bring them into focus.

2. Use the following script. Remember to pause frequently, allowing participants' images to form.

"Close your eyes and find a comfortable position for your entire body. Breathe in and out several times. Notice the rhythm of your breathing. Go back to a time when you remember feeling 'different.' If you can, go back to a childhood memory. How old were you? Where were you? What were you doing? Who else was there? What was that person like? Did anyone say anything to you or to someone else? What did they say or do? How did you respond? How did you feel?

"Now remember a more recent time when you felt 'different.' Where were you? Did anyone say or do anything? How did you respond or react? How did you feel? Finally, I want you to remember a time when you heard someone whose opinion you respected say something hurtful, harmful, or stereotypic about a 'different' individual or group. The remark could have come from a member of your family, community, church, synagogue, mosque, or school. What was said? What was your reaction? How did the information mesh with your reality? What did you say or do?

"Slowly, begin to return to the present. Remember this building, this room, your seat, and the people around you. I am going to ask you to share your images within a small group. When you are ready, open your eyes."

3. Ask participants to form groups of two to four members each. In their small groups, they are to discuss their personal images and memories, noting how earlier experiences have influenced the persons they have become. Ask them to share how their reactions to being or feeling "different" have changed as they have grown older.

4. Reconvene the entire group. Find three to five participants who are willing to share with the entire group. Form a panel of those volunteers and, with your help as a moderator, let these highly personal stories be told.

5. Obtain reactions to hearing and/or presenting these disclosures. Ask whether it was better to keep them locked away or to reveal them.

# Other Options ——————————————————

1. As an experiment, have half the group do the imagery without closing their eyes. Compare the experiences of those who did and those who did not. Expect that those who closed their eyes will report that their memories were more intense than those with eyes open.

2. Use "experiential writing." Instead of visualization, have participants write about a memory as if it were occurring in the present instead of the past.

# 8 FACILITATING TEAMS ‎‎‎‎—————————

# 36 Multi-Voting: A Constructive Way to Make Decisions

## Introductory Remarks

Multi-voting is an efficient and effective way to narrow the choices from a long list of decision options. Once the list is narrowed, it is often easier to obtain consensus. The members of the group prepare a list of possible solutions to a complex problem and are permitted to narrow the list themselves by casting a specified number of votes until only a few possibilities, those acceptable to the majority of the voters, remain. This eliminates the loss of many good ideas, one of the problems created by a single vote on a long list of items. This technique is more likely to keep those second-tier ideas viable. In this activity, participants experience this technique and evaluate its effectiveness.

## *Objectives*

- To experience a way to use voting as a constructive way to make decisions.

- To improve a group's chances of building a consensus.

**Group Size:** any

**Time Required:** 10 to 30 minutes

## *Materials*

- Paper ballots

- Flip chart and markers

# *Activity Flow*

1. On a flip chart, list any problem relevant to the group you are training that could be solved or lessened in different ways. Then share with the group some of those ways. Alternatively, you can use the following situation:

   A medium-size city is facing financial difficulties and must reduce costs. Proposals made thus far include:

   - Reduce the police force by 4 percent
   - Close some libraries
   - Increase classroom size from an average of twenty students to thirty
   - Raise the cost of parking meters by 40 percent
   - Eliminate health care benefits for city employees
   - Decrease garbage collection to once a week and recycling to every other week

2. Tell the participants to think carefully about which of the proposed solutions that they can accept.

3. Pass out ballots and ask the participants to vote for each proposal they find acceptable. *They should vote for as many as they want.* Inform them, however, that only alternatives receiving one-half of all the possible votes will remain in contention and be placed on a second ballot to be voted on after more discussion.

4. Collect the votes and tally the responses. Eliminate any choices that did not receive at least half the possible votes.

5. Hold a discussion of the remaining choices. Then vote again. The alternatives that receive at least one-half of all the possible votes on the second ballot remain on the list.

6. Determine at this point whether more voting is needed to narrow the choices to begin working on a consensus.

# Other Options

1. Have all the members write down those cost-reducing options they like best. Let them select up to one-third of the items on the list. For example, if there are fifteen items on the list, a participant may select up to five. Members can vote by a show of hands or, if the need for secrecy matters, on paper ballots.

   - Count the hands or collect the ballots and reduce the list by removing those options that received very few votes. (The number of votes will, of course, depend on the size of the group. For a small group, one or two votes may be the determining number for removal. If the group is fifteen or more, perhaps four or five votes would make a good cutoff number.)

   - Repeat these steps as often as necessary until only a few items remain.

   - At this point, if no clear favorite is apparent, have the group discuss which is the best choice and then take one last vote.

2. Have participants suggest their own multi-voting process.

# 37 Rotating Facilitators: Practicing Effective Facilitation

## Introductory Remarks

In this activity, participants have the experience of both observing others and practicing facilitation skills themselves. I created the ten skills list for *101 Ways to Make Training Active*. Rather than have participants simply read the checklist, I wanted a way for participants to learn it "experientially" by watching it, doing it, and debriefing it. The result is this activity.

## Objectives

- To provide skill practice in facilitation.
- To obtain feedback on one's facilitation skills.

**Group Size:** at least five participants
**Time Required:** 60 to 90 minutes

## Materials

- One copy of the Rotating Facilitators Ten Skills Checklist for each participant
- A prop to identify the current facilitator in each subgroup, such as a hat, badge, or Hawaiian lei.

# *Activity Flow*

1. Distribute the Rotating Facilitators Ten Skills Checklist. Ask participants to review the ten skills listed and to identify those that need more clarification. Also invite them to identify their reactions to the skills (for example, one they find uncomfortable, challenging). They should not complete the assessment portion at this time. Explain that you will be soliciting their reactions to the advice given on the handout.

2. Now ask participants to share their questions and reactions to the skills list. As you respond to participants, demonstrate as many of the ten facilitation skills as possible (for example, paraphrase someone's comments). After a while, ask participants to use the list to identify which skills you just used.

3. Arrange participants into groups of five to six participants. Explain that each group will work on an assigned task for the next 25 to 30 minutes. Each participant will take a 5-minute turn as the facilitator. When a participant's turn occurs, that person should try to use as many of the ten skills from the list as possible. Urge other group members to refrain from using any of the facilitative behaviors when it is not their turn.

4. Give each subgroup a task that relates to their own work situations or ask them to simulate a group with one of the following assignments:

   ▪ Developing creative ideas to deal with the problem of homelessness

   ▪ Marketing a new gourmet cookie business

   ▪ Improving customer service at . . . (any known company or organization)

   ▪ Creating a plan for faculty accountability in colleges and universities

5. Provide some creative way to identify the facilitator in each group, such as a hat, badge, or Hawaiian lei. Request that someone in each group volunteer to be the first facilitator.

6. Keep track of the time, announce when each 5-minute turn is over, and request that the person to the left of the current facilitator assume the role for the next 5 minutes. Rotate around the group until everyone has

taken a turn as facilitator. *Note:* you may wish to switch topics when you switch facilitators.

7.  Ask participants to complete the assessment portion of the checklist. Invite group members to share their assessments with one another.

8.  Debrief the activity by asking the following questions of the total group:

    - Which facilitation behaviors were the most difficult to use?

    - On which behaviors do you personally want to improve?

    - Which behaviors were more useful at the beginning, middle, and closing periods of the task?

# Other Options

1.  Create an open discussion period in which no one is formally designated the facilitator and then keep track of who uses which techniques.

2.  Ask participants to create their own list of facilitation skills. Then compare the list to the Ten Skills Checklist.

# *Rotating Facilitators Ten Skills Checklist*

*Instructions:* First read through the following list of ten facilitation skills. Decide whether any need to be clarified and whether you think the list is complete as it stands. When told to do so, decide whether you or others in your group practiced each of the facilitation skills or whether you need to practice a particular skill. Circle the appropriate phrase below each of the skills listed.

1.  **Paraphrase** what a participant has said so that he or she feels understood and so that the other participants can hear a concise summary of what has been said.

    Skill I Used          Skill Others Used          Skill I Need to Learn to Use

2.  **Check understanding** of a participant's statement or ask the participant to clarify what he or she is saying.

    Skill I Used          Skill Others Used          Skill I Need to Learn to Use

3.  **Compliment** an interesting or insightful comment.

    Skill I Used          Skill Others Used          Skill I Need to Learn to Use

4.  **Elaborate** on a participant's contribution to the discussion with examples or suggest a new way to view the problem.

    Skill I Used          Skill Others Used          Skill I Need to Learn to Use

5.  **Energiz**e a discussion by quickening the pace, using humor, or, if necessary, prodding the group for more contributions.

    Skill I Used          Skill Others Used          Skill I Need to Learn to Use

6. **Disagree** (gently) with a participant's comments to stimulate further discussion.

   Skill I Used          Skill Others Used          Skill I Need to Learn to Use

7. **Mediate** differences of opinion between participants and relieve any tensions that may be brewing.

   Skill I Used          Skill Others Used          Skill I Need to Learn to Use

8. **Pull together** ideas, showing their relationships to each other.

   Skill I Used          Skill Others Used          Skill I Need to Learn to Use

9. **Change** the group process by altering the method for obtaining participation or by having the group evaluate ideas that have been presented.

   Skill I Used          Skill Others Used          Skill I Need to Learn to Use

10. **Summarize** (and record, if desired) the key views of the group.

    Skill I Used          Skill Others Used          Skill I Need to Learn to Use

**Card Exchange: A Unique Way to Stimulate Discussion**

## Introductory Remarks

This activity is a clever strategy to share with team facilitators to help a medium to large group of people exchange ideas and opinions about issues that concern them. It is based on a strategy developed by Sivasailam "Thiagi" Thiagarajan. I like the activity because everyone is involved in a small team. Furthermore, each team uses the input of the entire group to solve a problem.

## *Objectives*

- To learn a technique in which participants exchange ideas in writing.
- To envision many ways to apply the technique.

**Group Size:** any

**Time Required:** 25 to 30 minutes

## *Materials*

- Prepared index cards (see Step 1)
- Two blank index cards for each participant
- (Optional) Newsprint and markers for each subgroup

## *Activity Flow*

1. Choose an issue or problem that an intact team is facing. If your participants are from different teams, select an issue that you would assume
   all the participants face. Before the process starts, prepare several index
   cards on which you have written some possible solutions to the issue/
   problem. Prepare about as many cards as there are participants and hold
   them in reserve.

   Here are some ideas that might diminish the financial difficulties facing
   an organization:

   ■ Don't waste money by sending out unnecessary mailings. Use email
     exclusively.

   ■ Accept that debt is normal, natural, and necessary for any growing
     organization.

   ■ Keep to a strict budget.

   ■ Sell some physical assets to build cash flow.

2. Hand out two blank index cards to each participant. Ask each participant
   to come up with two ways to address the issue you have chosen and to
   write one on each of the cards. Encourage them to be honest. Explain
   that the cards will be anonymous.

3. Collect the cards and shuffle them well into your prepared cards. Then
   randomly distribute to each participant three cards. Tell them to examine the cards and to arrange them in order of preference. Then instruct
   them to mill around the room exchanging cards in order to obtain a set
   of three they are happy with. Call time after 5 minutes. (If some participants complain about the cards they presently hold, tell them "relief is on
   the way.")

4. Arrange people in trios and have them select the three cards they prefer
   as a group. Ask them to discard cards they don't want and place them
   in a spot accessible to every trio. Any trio can rummage through the discarded cards to find any they prefer over the ones they have. Call time
   after 10 minutes.

5. Invite each group to give a short report on the statements they have chosen. (Consider giving each trio a sheet of newsprint to display their chosen statements.)

6. Have the entire group reflect on the commonalties and diversity of viewpoints among the subgroups.


# Other Options

1. This process can also be used to generate and discuss suggestions for change, factors that may be creating problems, or creative ideas for new initiatives.

2. Extend the process by continuing through to an actual decision.

# 39 The Problem with Majority Voting: A Double Whammy

## Introductory Remarks

This activity is what I call a "double whammy." Simultaneously, participants are combining the content and the process. In this case, the subject matter is "the problem with majority voting." While discussing this topic, participants are engaged in the preferred process of "reaching consensus."

## Objectives

- To examine the downsides of using majority voting as a decision-making practice.

- To experience reaching a consensus.

**Group Size:** at least eight participants

**Time Required:** 20 minutes

## Materials

- One copy of the Reaching Consensus handout for each participant

## Activity Flow

1. Explain that groups have options in making decisions—from voting to building consensus. Each option has advantages and disadvantages. Say that most experts agree that voting is among the most problematic.

2.  Recruit a group of four volunteers and ask them to agree on the best answer they can give to this question:

    ■ What is the major disadvantage to making decisions by majority voting?

3.  Tell them that they have up to 10 minutes to reach a decision. As they deliberate, give the rest of the participants the following observation questions:

    ■ Do the members of the volunteer group listen carefully to each other?

    ■ Does anyone change her or his position just to keep peace?

    ■ Do they explore alternative ideas?

    ■ Do they resolve differences through discussion or compromise?

    ■ Is consensus actively sought by some form of verbal polling or is it assumed that everyone agrees?

4.  After the 10-minute deliberation is over, have the observers present feedback to the volunteers about what they observed.

5.  Distribute the handout, Reaching Consensus. If time permits, have participants read it and discuss the contents. If not, suggest that they read it on their own.

# Other Options

1.  Recruit four to six participants who will begin the planning for the end-of-the-year company party. Give them 10 minutes to reach a decision on the major goals of the party. Ask observers to comment on how they went about reaching a decision: minority rule (the most outspoken decided), majority vote, or building a group-wise consensus. What were the consequences of the process used? In what way could a quality decision emerge?

2.  Discuss suggestions that participants have on how to build consensus without endlessly long meetings and/or unresolved conflict.

# *Reaching Consensus*

Which of the following suggestions would be useful to the teams you facilitate?

1. If your team is large and reaching a total consensus would be difficult, establish a prior ground rule that any decision reached by a team must have the agreement of a super-majority of the group (for example, 75 percent).

2. After some discussion of an issue, take a "straw poll" of members to capture the relative strength of various decision options. Explain that the straw poll is not a binding vote. Its only purpose is to provide a snapshot of where the team is relative to a decision.

3. Provide team members who are in the minority on an issue with the opportunity to be heard without debate from the majority. Sometimes, providing this opportunity for "dissenting opinions" allows dissenters to go along with a majority without feeling that they were disregarded.

4. Use a process by which the team weighs each remaining decision option against a set of criteria, such as cost, ease of implementation, best reward/cost ratio, and so forth. Such a discussion tends to be more objective.

5. Put a decision "on trial." Suggest that any decision reached is "on trial" for a period of time to evaluate its effectiveness. After the trial period is over, the decision is reviewed.

# 40 Changing the Rules: Altering Group Process

## Introductory Remarks

Ever been a facilitator in a situation where a group gets into little squabbles, locks horns, or goes in circles? You need to do something dramatic to alter the climate. In this activity, some possible interventions are experienced and debriefed by the participants. Each involves the use of a "rule" that the group agrees to follow as it continues to discuss the issue that has not been resolved.

## *Objectives*

- To experience different discussion "rules."
- To assess the impact of these "rules."

**Group Size:** sixteen participants or fewer

**Time Required:** 30 minutes

## *Materials*

- Four marking pens and four sheets of newsprint

## *Activity Flow*

1. Tell participants to imagine a meeting about the upcoming office holiday party. Participants have very different views . . . some want games with fun

prizes for the winners, some want skits that spoof daily office events, and some want a serious presentation of this year's achievements. In the last several minutes, the discussion has really deteriorated and no progress toward a decision has been made. As a concerned member of the planning committee, you want to try something to see whether it will help move things along.

2. Explain that you would like to have everyone abide by a series of stringent ground rules over the next 20 minutes. Each is designed to change the way meeting participants are interacting with one another.

3. In 5-minute rounds, let the group experience each of the following rule changes:

   ■ As each person speaks, each person must express what he or she likes about other people's ideas without, he or she must first *paraphrase* what the previous speaker said.

   ■ Each speaker must *own* (take personal responsibility for) what he or she is saying. The speaker cannot speak for others and must insert "in my opinion" or "here's what I think" before speaking.

   ■ Participants must say what they *like* about another's idea before giving any criticism or additional ideas.

   ■ Questions only are allowed. Participants listen to what questions are on others' minds. No replies are given until every participant has had a chance to ask a question.

4. When this process is completed, post four sheets of newsprint, one identifying each of the four rules. Display the four rules around the room. Place a marking pen near each rule. Ask participants to circulate around the room and write brief comments on the impact of each rule (such as "forced us to listen very carefully to people with whom we disagreed").

5. Review the comment sheets one at a time with the participants.

6. Do a final debriefing, asking participants to select rule changes that have the best shot at success for them when facilitating a group discussion.

# Other Options

1.  Select only one of the rules and allow it to remain in effect for 15 minutes. Assess the impact.

2.  Conduct a group discussion on any topic for at least 20 minutes. Give these four "suggestions" (rather than applying "rules"):

    - Paraphrase what the preceding speaker has said
    - "Own" what you say
    - Express what you like about other people's ideas
    - Ask questions of others

# 41 Removing Egos: A Tool for Team Facilitators

─────**Introductory Remarks**─────

Often, a team's process is hurt by participants who are self-centered and domineering. This process is a discreet way to shrink over-sized egos to standard group size. It is also very effective at minimizing endless group debate. The process encourages participation from everyone but tends to discourage any single participant from dominating the group. Facilitators may be familiar with *the nominal group technique.* Below, you will find a simplified version of this technique that should bring similar results.

## Objectives

- To demonstrate a technique that examines problem solving and idea generation without knowing the author of any specific contribution.
- To practice the use of this technique in real-life situations.

**Group Size:** ten to twenty-five participants

**Time Required:** over 30 minutes

## Materials

- Eight to ten index cards and a pen/pencil for each participant
- Flip chart and markers

# *Activity Flow*

1. Explain to participants that you will be using a procedure that allows ideas to be evaluated without knowing who contributed them. This is done to maximize group decision making and minimize individual politicking.

2. Follow these steps.

   - State a task clearly and succinctly. Choose from these sample tasks or create your own.

     - A task force is charged with developing ideas for new goals and initiatives in the next two years for a local charity organization

     - A team is creating ground rules for discussion by which it will abide

     - A committee is to make two recommendations on how to improve employee morale

   - Ask each participant to write his or her ideas about how to accomplish the task on index cards *in silence*. They may write as many ideas as they like (one idea per card).

   - Collect the cards. Reshuffle the cards and distribute them to a card reader. Do not allow discussion at this point; have the reader read aloud each card and list the idea it contains on a flip chart. Assign a number to each suggestion. (Ask participants not to reveal who contributed a specific idea.) Promote the notion that all the ideas are now the "property of the group."

   - Next, allow the individuals to discuss all the ideas listed, clarifying or condensing them. Discourage outright lobbying.

   - Give a new index card to each person. Have each participant write "First Vote" in a corner of the card and have him or her rank the top five ideas, giving a score of 5 to the top-ranked idea, 4 to the next ranked, and so forth. Total the scores for each idea and arrange the ideas in the order of their scores—highest to lowest.

   - Have the group debate the items on the list a second time.

- Have the meeting participants label a fresh card "Second Vote" and write on it three to five of the ideas they favor without consulting with the others.

- Tally the final rankings and clarify each one for the participants so that everyone understands the final decisions.

3. Ask participants to share situations from their own teams, units, or organizations for which this process might be helpful. Allow three volunteers to choose one situation and to role play the process with other participants. Obtain feedback.

# Other Options

1. Ask participants: "What would be the ideal course of action we could take to satisfy all of the viewpoints in our group?" Focusing on this question may also be a way to remove egos from the matter at hand.

2. Discuss the difference between *advocating* an idea and *offering* one. Teach the notion that members of a team offer ideas with the following words: "I offer to the group the idea that we. . . ."

# 9 EXCHANGING FEEDBACK

# 42 Animal Metaphors: An Exercise in Obtaining Honest Feedback

## Introductory Remarks

In this exercise, participants are asked to identify an animal that describes a co-participant. What I like about this activity are its surprises. When doing training on feedback, asking participants to choose an animal that comes to mind in describing another person startles them. At first, it seems like fun, but most participants realize that their choices and the reasons for them can be just as serious business as finding words that convey one's perceptions of another person. The second surprise concerns the polling questions asked by the facilitator before any animal is revealed. After completing all the steps of the exercise, I have often witnessed its impact on the participants. I remember a participant who was actually shaken by the realization that she had rarely if ever asked for (rather than waited for) honest feedback from the people closest to her.

## *Objectives*

- To demonstrate why people often don't obtain honest feedback.
- To identify alternative strategies to obtain honest feedback from others.

**Group Size:** any size

**Time Required:** 20 to 30 minutes

# Materials

- One copy of the Animal Metaphors handout for each participant

- One copy of the Ways to Encourage Feedback from Others handout for each participant

- One copy of the Requesting Feedback handout for each participant

# Activity Flow

1. Form participants into pairs. (It does not matter if the partners know each other or are strangers.) Distribute the Animal Metaphors handout and ask participants to take 1 minute to select animals that best describe their partners and to develop reasons for their choices. *Caution participants not to reveal their selections yet.*

2. When 1 minute has expired, state the following: "Before you tell your partner the animal you have chosen, I have two questions for you." The first question is: "How many of you are eager to tell your partner the animal you've chosen?" (Observe the number and speed with which people raise their hands.) Then ask: "How many of you are eager to find out what animal your partner has chosen?" (You should notice after this question that more people raise their hands and do so with greater enthusiasm.) Highlight these key points:

    - People usually prefer to *receive* feedback rather than to *give* it. It's difficult to give honest feedback because you may be afraid to say something that is not helpful or, worse, is hurtful.

    - Because of this fact, very little feedback is given between people. If nearly everyone wants to *receive* feedback more than *give* it, nearly everyone will *not* receive any feedback—except for mandated performance appraisals.

3. State the following: "Now, it's time to find out from your partner the animal he or she has chosen and the reasoning behind the choice . . . but instead of just telling each other this information, I want each of you to INVITE your partner to reveal it. Your job is

to ask for the animal feedback in such a way that your partner feels ENCOURAGED to tell you. Say something so that your partner feels that you really want the feedback and that it's safe for him or her to be honest."

4.  Allow 5 minutes for partners to invite and receive the animal feedback from each other.

5.  Debrief the activity by asking a few participants to share with the entire group how their partners "encouraged" them to reveal the feedback. (Ask: "How many of you would like to 'brag' about your partner's skill in making you feel eager to tell him or her the 'animal feedback'?")

6.  Distribute the Ways to Encourage Feedback handout and give participants time to review the six suggestions. Invite comments and questions.

7.  Next, distribute the Requesting Feedback handout to participants. Request that they fill out the list of names first and then await further instructions.

8.  When participants have listed a few names, ask them to select one person from whom they would like to receive feedback and to specify the type of feedback they are seeking from that person.

9.  Now ask participants to review the strategies on the Ways to Encourage Feedback handout and select one or more they would like to use to encourage feedback from the person they have identified. Have them complete the last section of the Requesting Feedback handout.

10. Conclude the activity by inviting one or two participants to share their plans to encourage feedback. Urge participants to act on their own plans in the near future.

# Other Options

1.  When conducting this activity with participants who know and work with each other, eliminate the use of animal metaphors. Instead, ask each

participant to prepare some verbal feedback about his or her partner as a team member. Use the same directions as above.

2. Consider using animal metaphors as a playful way for participants to assess themselves. For example, a person might say to a partner: "Most of my life I've been a kind of 'teddy bear,' a friendly, soft, and approachable person who wanted to be 'wanted' by others. Right now, my goal is to be more of a lion, with a strong, independent persona that gains the respect of others, without intimidation."

# *Animal Metaphors*

*Instructions:* From the list below, select the animal that most resembles your partner, considering both physical characteristics and personal qualities you perceive about your partner. Please make your selection even if you have no prior familiarity with your partner.

DO NOT TELL YOUR PARTNER YOUR SELECTION UNTIL YOU ARE TOLD TO DO SO. THINK ABOUT HOW YOU WILL EXPLAIN YOUR CHOICE TO YOUR PARTNER.

| | |
|---|---|
| **LION** | **SQUIRREL** |
| **MONKEY** | **DOLPHIN** |
| **TIGER** | **GIRAFFE** |
| **KANGAROO** | **HORSE** |
| **BIRD** (specify type) | **BEAR** (specify type) |
| **CAT** (specify type) | **DOG** (specify type) |

# *Ways to Encourage Feedback from Others*

1. Present a sincere rationale for wanting their feedback.

   *I'm serious about improving my meeting facilitation skills, and you could really help me by sharing some of your thoughts about how I led our last meeting.*

2. Be specific about the feedback you're seeking.

   *Would you please tell me whether you have noticed me interrupting others?*

3. Give others time to prepare their feedback.

   *I'd really like your feedback about how I handled this presentation. Would you be willing to get back to me by the end of the week with your thoughts?*

4. Self-assess to start the process.

   *I thought I was pretty patient with Ron's objections, but I'm not sure I did a very good job supporting your views. What did you think?*

5. Make the feedback anonymous.

   *I'm asking several people for feedback on my performance as a computer consultant. Please respond to the questions below and return it to my mailbox anonymously.*

6. Suggestions only:

   *What do you think I could have done differently to try to close that sale?*

# *Requesting Feedback*

List below the names of people with whom you work:

Select someone from whom you would like to receive feedback and specify what you want feedback about from that person:

What strategies will you use to encourage feedback from that person?

# 43 Giving Effective Feedback: Wheaties Over Donuts

## Introductory Remarks

In this activity, participants experience a five-step model for giving effective feedback. They also try out the model themselves. This is another example of a "double whammy." Participants give each other feedback on their feedback-giving skills. It's an efficient way to maximize practice time.

## Objectives

- To acquaint participants with a five-step model for giving effective feedback.
- To practice the model and obtain feedback from peers.

**Group Size:** any

**Time Required:** 30 minutes

## Materials

- One copy of the Giving Feedback handout for each participant

## Activity Flow

1. Share with participants the phrase, *Feedback is the breakfast of champions.* Like breakfast, feedback is something that helps you grow.

2. Distribute the Giving Feedback handout to participants. Pair up participants.

3.  Instruct participants to discuss the tips with their partners.

4.  Point out that some feedback situations tend to be formal, while some are informal.

5.  Say: "While all these tips may not apply to every situation, which tips are you most 'guilty,' in your opinion, of not using?" Discuss responses.

6.  Say: "Giving feedback is different from asserting your needs. When you offer feedback, don't insist that the other person change. You only give the feedback because you want to share your perceptions and be helpful."

7.  Instruct participants to think of someone to whom they'd like to give feedback. It can be a person who reports to them or even a person to whom they report. It may also be to a colleague or a current client/customer.

8.  Demonstrate giving feedback with a volunteer. Ask the volunteer to describe his or her situation. Role play with the volunteer and show how he or she can give the person feedback effectively, with the facilitator showing how to give good feedback and the volunteer acting as the person to whom he or she wishes to give feedback.

9.  Ask participants to identify how you used the tips in the Giving Feedback handout.

10. Instruct participants to pretend their partners are the people they chose and practice giving their feedback. Partners should then use the checklist from the handout to describe how effective the feedback was. Each partner should take a turn practicing giving feedback. (*If time is short, do a single round in which just one partner gets a chance to practice giving feedback.*) Conclude with feedback to one's partner using the feedback checklist.

11. Debrief by inviting one or two participants to share which strategies they used.

# Other Options

1.  Select a celebrity most in the group would know well and to whose actions participants have personal reactions. Examples are the current

president of the United States, a person in the entertainment business, or a professional athlete. Assume the role of that person and invite participants to role play giving feedback to that celebrity. To allow several people to practice, do one step at a time (for example, asking permission), and then rotate to a new role player.

2. Ask participants to think of someone to whom they have recently given negative feedback. If they did not give the person suggestions for improvement, write down two things that the person could do to improve. Say: "When you next have an opportunity to speak with the person, tell him or her, 'I've been thinking about the feedback I gave you the other day, and I'm not sure I was as helpful as I could have been. Could I take a moment to explain more clearly what I meant, and try to give you some concrete suggestions?' If the person agrees, give your improved feedback, then check out whether this was helpful to the person."

# *Giving Feedback*

1. Discuss the checklist below with your partner:

   ☐ Ask permission.
   - "Can we talk about what happened between us at the meeting?"
   - "I have some things I'd like to say to you. Is this a good time?"

   ☐ Compliment first.
   - "I appreciate your. . . ."
   - "I like the way you. . . ."

   ☐ Talk to the behavior or action, not the person. Be specific.
   - "I'm concerned about the way you handled your sales call. You focused on the features of the product but not on the benefits."

   ☐ Offer suggestions.
   - "I'd like to suggest that you. . . ."
   - "I think I/you/we would be more effective if you. . . ."

   ☐ Ask for reactions.
   - "Is this helpful?"
   - "How do you see it?"

2. Choose someone from your work environment to whom you'd like to give feedback.

3. Pretend your partner is that person and practice giving him or her constructive feedback.

4. Using the points on the checklist below as a guide, tell your partner how effective his or her feedback was.

**Feedback Checklist**

☐ Asked permission?

☐ Complimented first?

☐ Talked to the behavior or action, not the person?

☐ Was specific?

☐ Offered suggestions?

☐ Asked for reactions?

# **44** **Judging the Impact of Words: Applications to Giving Feedback**

## Introductory Remarks

One of the challenges of giving feedback effectively is
to match what you are saying to how you are saying it.
People can see and hear the same thing very differently,
depending on how the words are perceived. In this activity,
a feedback session is heard word for word. However, the
participants listening to it often have different perceptions
of its impact. I like this activity because it debunks the
idea of a single ideal way of doing something.

## *Objectives*

- To study and apply well-known criteria for useful feedback.

- To demonstrate that feedback comments are in the eyes and ears
  of the beholder.

**Group Size:** any

**Time Required:** 20 minutes

## *Materials*

- One copy of An Example of Performance Feedback for each volunteer

- One copy of What Makes Feedback Useful for each of the remaining
  participants

## *Activity Flow*

1. Obtain two volunteers to read a script containing a dialogue between two people, which is provided on the An Example of Performance Feedback handout. Give them a private space to practice so that it is read smoothly when it is presented to the entire group.

2. While they are rehearsing, distribute the What Makes Feedback Useful? handout. Discuss and clarify each criterion.

3. Now, invite the two volunteers to enact the feedback exchange. Tell the other participants to look for instances in which one or more of the criteria are met during the feedback session.

4. Ask each of the volunteers to identify positive feedback behaviors (without having seen the What Makes Feedback Useful handout).

5. Now, open up the assessment to the entire group. You should find that, from a technical point of view, the quality of the feedback is quite good. However, expect that many of your participants will differ in their conclusions because of differences in how they felt about the words used. Check whether this is true in your group.

6. Use this disparity in opinion as a segue into discussing how many factors, such as voice tone, affect the impact of what is said. Relate this consideration to other areas of communication besides giving feedback.

7. Ask all the participants what they are taking away from the activity.

## **Other Options**

1. Invite participants to brainstorm nonverbal factors that affect how feedback is achieved. Include these categories: voice, posture, and facial expressions.

2. Invite participants to dramatize each factor presented in the What Makes Feedback Useful handout, using both positive and negative examples.

# *An Example of Performance Feedback*

Scenario: Roberta (or Robert), a pharmaceutical sales trainer, has accompanied a new trainee-representative, Sam (or Samantha), on his (or her) sales calls. The two called on four physicians this morning and five physicians this afternoon. It's near the end of the day, and the trainer suggests that they stop for coffee and a debriefing session before they call it a day.
Instructions: As the two volunteers read the following role play, please observe carefully and take note of

(1) What the trainer does well in providing feedback and (2) In what ways he or she could improve.

R: It's been a pretty exhausting afternoon, hasn't it?

S: Boy, I'll say! Some of these doctors can be really tough to sell.

R: Well, that's what I want to talk to you about. I thought this would be a good opportunity to give you some feedback on what I observed and also give you some suggestions to help your calls go more smoothly. After all, both your goal and mine is to help you make more sales. Right?

S: Absolutely. Okay, let me have it.

R: Let me start by saying that I think one of your biggest assets is that you are very warm and friendly. That really helps in establishing rapport with the customer. You have a great personality, and you do a great job of creating rapport with the doctors.

S: That's good to know. I've been told that I have the gift of gab and can sell anything to anybody.

R: You certainly have the talent. All we need to do now is to fine-tune your selling skills. One of the things you have going for you is that you seem to know the products well. It's obvious that you're well versed on the features and benefits of each product. You do a good job of getting the main points across in a very limited amount of time. Do you agree?

S: Absolutely. I'm really confident that I know the products.

R: Since product knowledge is not a problem, we need to take a look at what is getting in the way of a really successful sales call. The biggest thing I notice is that in your eagerness and enthusiasm, you aren't taking enough time to plan your sales call. As a result, you come across as disorganized and unprepared. That's one thing. The second problem I see is that you seem to be a little too eager to close the sale based on one or two of the physician's needs instead of taking the time to identify and prioritize the physician's major needs. Do you know what I mean?

S: I'm not sure I do.

R: For one thing, you don't ask enough open-ended questions to uncover what the physician's most important needs really are. Because you know the products so well, you seem to focus on just telling the doctor about the products. I also think that you need to do a better job of really listening to what the doctor is telling you. I don't think you're picking up on the nonverbal cues. What I would recommend for your next set of calls is to do a better job of pre-planning, including the preparation of some open probes. During the call, concentrate on asking open-ended questions and really listening to the doctor's responses; that includes body language as well. Other than those few things, I think you're doing a good job. So, do you think you can work on those things I just mentioned?

S: Well . . . okay.

R: Good. I'm sure you'll see a big difference the next time out.

# *What Makes Feedback Useful*

Useful feedback is . . .

☐ Descriptive rather than evaluative.

☐ Detailed and specific.

☐ Constructive (it informs and enlightens).

☐ Directed toward behavior that can be changed.

☐ Well-timed.

☐ Checked to ensure clear communication.

# 45 When Asking for or Giving Feedback Is Challenging: Your Advice

## Introductory Remarks

Asking for or giving feedback is not without its challenges. In this activity, participants have the opportunity to deal with four concrete situations, each having its own challenges. I have found that participants come away from this activity with a greater confidence in exchanging feedback.

## *Objectives*

- To confront situations that are not expected to be feedback sessions.
- To gain confidence in being able to handle a variety of feedback challenges.

**Group Size:** at least twelve

**Time Required:** 40 minutes

## *Materials*

- One copy of the Four Scenarios handout for each participant

## *Activity Flow*

1. Explain that giving feedback at expected moments such as a performance review differs from situations in which the other party is not expecting

anything. This activity will deal with these unexpected opportunities for either asking for or giving feedback.

2. Divide participants into four subgroups. Distribute the Four Scenarios handout.

3. Ask participants to find a volunteer to be a discussion leader for each of the four scenarios on the handout. The goal is to discuss each scenario in two ways: (1) What are the challenges in the situation? and (2) How would you advise handling each situation? Allot 10 minutes for the discussion.

4. When the previous step is completed, ask the subgroups to dramatize each of the scenarios in a 5-minute demonstration.

5. Reconvene the entire group. Obtain a team willing to share its dramatization and obtain feedback on the drama. Follow this process until all four scenarios are dramatized.

6. Beyond discussing each of the concrete situations, ask the entire group to share the general insights they have obtained and any lessons they have learned from the entire process.

# Other Options

1. Invite participants to dramatize situations of their own choosing.

2. Ask participants to reduce their advice for each situation to one sentence. Have them display their advice on newsprint for all to see.

# *Four Scenarios*

Here are some scenarios that challenge your skill at asking for or giving feedback.

## 1. *When a Direct Report Needs Grooming*

"I'm an office administrator and one of the support staff I supervise is just not fitting in. Sally is a hard worker and, basically, a good person, but her dress and behavior are often inappropriate and unprofessional. She wears low-cut blouses, mini-skirts, or tight pants and a lot of makeup. Her language would fit better in a locker room than a boardroom. I've heard her co-workers talk about her disparagingly and I feel like it's my responsibility to say something to her. But how do I talk to her about something as personal as her grooming without getting her angry or upset?"

## 2. *Dealing with Gossip*

"I overheard one of my direct reports, Jerry, talking to a co-worker and making some very disparaging remarks about another member of the team, Lou. How do I discuss this with Jerry?"

## 3. *Opening a "Clam"*

"One of my direct reports just won't open up and share opinions, even when I ask. Her favorite response is 'I don't know.' Her work is good, so I know she's not stupid. How can I get more input from her?"

## 4. *Handling a Chronic Complainer*

"Someone on my staff is extremely negative. He responds to every request with a complaint, even in team meetings. Everyone notices his behavior and it's having a negative effect on morale. What can I do?"

# 10 LEADERSHIP ⸺

## 46 | The Window Shade: Depicting Different Approaches to Decision Making

**─────Introductory Remarks─────**

This activity utilizes a drawing of three window shades. Each depicts a different approach to how a leader makes decisions. Using this visual, participants can easily observe effective and ineffective models for their own leadership. What helps this activity is its open manner. Participants can discuss their approaches without being defensive.

## Objectives

- To visualize three different approaches to decision making.
- To encourage honest reflection about leadership style.

**Group Size:** any

**Time Required:** 15 minutes

## Materials

- A copy of The Window Shade of Decision Making handout for each participant
- A blank sheet of paper for each participant

## Activity Flow

1. Explain that an effective way to conceptualize the control of upper levels of leadership in some organizations is to compare their decision-making

power to a window shade. Initiative at lower levels is often inhibited when the shade is drawn too far down. It is even worse when the window shade is drawn differently every day. In this instance, initiative is further inhibited because middle managers and supervisors are continually confused about where their areas of responsibility lie.

2. Distribute the Window Shade of Decision Making handout to each participant.

3. Ask participants to give examples of decision making in which the window shade is too far down. Have them identify the kinds of decisions that dampen initiative.

4. Next, form small teams and ask them to create case scenarios in which the window shade constantly shifts. Have them present their scenarios.

5. Finally, state that the window shade should ideally be consistent. Where it is drawn depends on the situation. Have teams illustrate the appropriate length of the window shade in two different situations on newsprint or whiteboard. For example, a commanding officer in the military might keep the window shade fairly low, but leaders in a creative technology company might want to keep it high to empower their employees.

6. Obtain reactions to using the Window Shade of Decision Making model.

7. Have participants draw their own window shades. The first drawing should be the current way in which they make decisions. The second drawing should reflect any changes they plan to make in the future.

8. Have participants display and explain their drawings.

# Other Options

1. Ask participants, meeting in small groups of three or four, to use others in the group for feedback about their drawings and to ask for their advice, if any.

2. Ask participants to brainstorm other ways to depict decision-making styles visually.

# *The Window Shade of Decision Making*

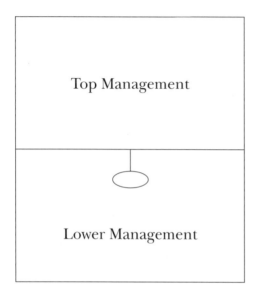
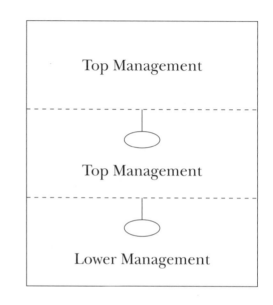

**Mirroring: Experiencing the Joys and Tribulations of Being a Leader**

## Introductory Remarks

This simple exercise can do a lot. Asking participants to be exercise leaders for fellow participants quickly gets participants into an experience that generates both positive and negative feelings about leadership. Moreover, participants have a lot of fun and learn a very basic lesson about leadership they are not likely to forget.

## *Objectives*

- To experience oneself in a leadership situation.
- To identify advantages and disadvantages of being a leader.
- To learn that effective leadership combines competence and consideration.

**Group Size:** any

**Time Required:** 10 minutes

## *Materials*

- One copy of the Job Ad handout for each participant

# *Activity Flow*

1.  Have participants form pairs. If there is an odd number of people, become partners with the remaining participant. Designate the person whose first name comes earlier in the alphabet as the "leader." Designate the other person as the "follower."

2.  Obtain a volunteer "follower." Explain that the leader's role is to engage the follower in mirroring or imitating what the leader does *as* he or she stretches (for example, reaching one's hands as high as possible) or moves aerobically (for example, jumping jacks). Demonstrate the leader's role, clearly showing that the mirroring is simultaneous, not after each movement. In other words, the flow of motion is continuous.

3.  Inform the "leaders" that they are to begin and to keep going for 2 minutes.

4.  Stop and have the pairs reverse roles. Before saying "begin," request that the new leaders be original and not repeat what their partners did. Again, call time after 2 minutes.

5.  Let the participants sit down. Then ask: "What did you like about being the leader?" Expect responses such as: "I had control. I could dictate what we did and the speed with which we did it." Remark that being in a leadership position has its advantages.

6.  Next, ask: "What did you **not** like about being the leader? Did you have any concerns"? Expect responses such as: "I had to think! Be original! I was concerned whether my partner was comfortable with what I was doing. Was I a good role model?" Remark that being in a leadership position has its challenges. It is a job with special demands and sensitivities. All leaders have similar concerns and challenges. Ask participants to share how this is true for them in real life.

7.  Distribute the Job Ad handout. Ask participants to compose a short ad for the ideal leader who would lead them in energizing movements every day. The ad might begin: Seeking someone who is. . . . When they are done, ask them the following: "Which attributes did you list that indicated that you want a person who is supportive and considerate?" Obtain several examples. Ask: "Which attributes did you list that indicated that

you want a person who is inspiring and competent?" Again, ask for examples. Expect attributes that pertain to both questions.

8. In real life, people want a combination package in their "bosses": bosses who know what they are doing, inspire, and give clear direction. They also want bosses who are approachable and reinforcing.

9. Ask: "Is this true for you?" "Is it true for people you lead?"

# Other Options

1. Review styles of leadership that are based on how leaders deal with both confidence and approachability. The best example is the Situational Leadership model that provides four styles: *directing, coaching, supporting,* and *empowering.*

2. Demonstrate or show video examples of how both aspects of leadership, confidence and approachability, can be integrated.

# *Job Ad*

*Instructions:* Complete the following ad for finding someone who would be your daily energizer.

Seeking someone who:

_____

_____

_____

_____

_____

_____

# 48 Going Outside Comfort Zones: Brief Exercises in Change

## Introductory Remarks

There is a joke that "nobody likes a change except a wet baby." By the time we are adults, we develop very persistent ways of doing things. The "habits" allow us to stay in our comfort zones, where we can be on "automatic pilot," not requiring a lot of thought and effort. This exercise is an adaptation of the well-known activity of asking people to interlace their fingers and then reversing the way they do it. This simple change immediately allows participants to experience change. I have made the experience more intense by using two other simple changes, separately and together.

## Objectives

- To experience resistance to change.
- To discuss how to help people to change.

**Group Size:** any

**Time Required:** 20 to 30 minutes

## Materials

- One copy of the Four Keys to Change handout for each participant

## *Activity Flow*

1. Say: "Here is a simple demonstration of something we do without thinking."

2. Instruct participants: "Fold your arms without thinking. Now fold them the opposite way so that you switch which arm is on top. Feel awkward? You bet. Well, stay that way for a minute. Now, if your legs are not already crossed, cross them without thinking about it. Yep, the upper part of your body is still uncomfortable, but your lower part is nice and comfortable. Now cross your legs the opposite way. All of you are now out of your comfort zones. So go right back to the way you fold your arms and cross your legs. Feel better now? Yep, that's the real you. Comfortable, but doing something the same way all the time!"

3. Explain that, for better or worse, we adults have gotten used to not only the ways we fold our arms or cross our legs, but to the ways we relate to other people. And it would be uncomfortable to change our ways.

4. Say: "Let's talk about some of the things we do habitually and would be reluctant to change. As we have this discussion, I would like you again to fold your arms the opposite way for you." (Pause). "Now, again cross your legs the opposite way for you." (Pause). "Please stay with these two new positions until I say you can stop."

5. Ask: "What are some things that, if you changed your way of doing them, would have little benefit, such as writing with the opposite hand?" Obtain responses for 2 minutes. (Don't allow participants to raise their hands to be recognized. Just let them call out their comments.) Next ask: "What are some things that, if you changed your way of doing things, might be beneficial, such as dribbling a basketball with either hand?" (Obtain responses for 2 minutes.)

6. Allow participants to return to any positions now that are comfortable. (Expect expressions of relief.)

7. Debrief the experience: "What were you feeling during this experience? Did you become more comfortable as time went on? More uncomfortable? What are some things that you would like to change even if it would be difficult?"

8. Conclude by saying that we are all resistant to change, and yet we can change. We all have certain restrictions; for example, with respect to our physical fitness, we are limited by our body type, genetic makeup, and age in terms of the physical prowess we can achieve. However, we can each still become much more physically fit than we presently are. Change will only happen if you do four things.

9. Distribute the Four Keys to Change handout. Allow participants a few minutes to read it. Discuss the handout, asking what advice sounds the most helpful to them as leaders.

## Other Options

1. Use the well-known exercise of changing the way you interlace your fingers by asking participants to slowly go back and forth from the usual way they do it to its opposite. As they do this back-and-forth process, ask them: "In which way do your fingers fit together 'like a glove'?" (The way they always do it.) "Contrast this with the extra space between your fingers and your palms the new way. Consider the fact that making a change allows you more space for change."

2. Try other changes. Here are some possibilities:

   - Change the usual finger or hand on which you usually wear a ring.
   - Wear something inside out, such as a watch, or turn around a necklace or bracelet.
   - Have a conversation with your eyes closed.
   - Add to or delete body language movements.

# *Four Keys to Change*

1. *You've got to WANT IT.* From the start, be honest with yourself and determine whether you want to make the change. You need to have specific goals in mind. You are more likely to be motivated if you are aware of when and where you need the skill the most. Don't go for a complete "makeover." Determine small steps that might help you to get started.

2. *You've got to LEARN IT.* Become familiar with ideas and suggestions you can read or talk about with people who can act as mentors and supporters. While you don't need a whole course in each area in which you would like to make a change, it is important to acquire a little knowledge and advice.

3. *You've got to TRY IT.* Most people make the mistake of going for broke and then fizzle out when results don't come quickly. Conduct an "experiment in change." Try on a small change in behavior for size and see whether you like what happens. Don't kid yourself. You won't persist unless you find that there is something in it for you. Test your wings and find the initial success to sustain yourself for further practice.

4. *You've got to LIVE IT.* One of the reasons that changes don't last is that, after people get pumped up about doing something, they try to make it on sheer inspiration and will power. They may make some headway, but then quickly relapse. Real change only comes by overcoming obstacles that are in the way in our daily life . . . not by jumping over buildings in leaping bounds. Confront *your* difficulties with making the change. It may be difficult for you for reasons that are different than for someone else. If you face the reasons why the change is difficult for you, you will have a greater chance of incorporating new growth into your life. If you live it, it works!

These steps apply to any area of self-improvement. For example, suppose you wanted to quit smoking. Even if you admit to yourself that it's a bad habit, you still have to really *want* to do something about it, especially if you enjoy smoking. Therefore, it may prove necessary to keep in mind specific situations in which your smoking bothers you, such as when you jog and feel short of breath, or when you find yourself watching the clock in a meeting because you want a cigarette. Next you might find it helpful to *learn* about the latest methods for quitting, such as nicotine patches or SmokeEnders groups. When you decide to *try* something different, it will feel like an "experiment in change" to get through a day without a cigarette. If the experiment is successful, you may then be able to build the approach you have been using into your lifestyle. You will start to *live* it. Along the way, there will be plenty of obstacles you will need to identify and find ways to overcome. If you do, the change will last.

## **49** Changes You Would Make: Dreaming Beyond the Status Quo

---
### Introductory Remarks

One of my goals when doing leadership training is to encourage the participants to stretch their thinking about changes they would like to see in their organization. This exercise never fails to unleash the capacity of each participant to be open to change.

---

## *Objectives*

- To reflect on possible new directions for one's organization.
- To begin the development of new initiatives.

**Group Size:** any

**Time Required:** 60 minutes

## *Materials*

- One copy of the Your Current Practices handout for each participant

## *Activity Flow*

1. Explain that any organization has its ways of doing things. Distribute the Your Current Practices handout and ask participants to look over the list as they think about the current status of affairs in their organizations.

2. Say: "Close your eyes. Breathe in and breathe out. . . . You are leaders in your organization. Where do you want to lead to? What changes would you like your organization to make? Imagine that there are no obstacles. You are dreaming up a wide range of possibilities. . . . Set aside your current concerns about 'the way things are.' Let your mind go. Consider big changes and little changes." (Pause for 3 minutes.) "Now open your eyes and get together with a partner and share some of the changes you thought about for the next 5 minutes. Don't go into too much detail. Don't explain the reasons for the changes, just the changes themselves."

3. Encourage all of the participants to share their ideas with the whole group, beginning with any of these phrase(s):

   - I wonder . . .

   - What if . . .

   - Maybe we . . .

   - I have a dream that . . .

   - If only we . . .

   - I wish . . .

   - Why can't we . . .

   Use a "go-around" format. Rotate around the room, allowing each participant to share one sentence. Insist that people listen but not respond to what is shared until several statements have been made.

4. Create groups of four to six participants. Ask each group to discuss the following:

   - What were some dreams other than your own that excite you? Why is that?

5. Have each group select one of the "dreams" from the preceding discussion. Tell them to convert the "dream" into a "proposal." Explain that each group will analyze its selected proposal using a popular method called a SWOT analysis. It focuses on four ways to evaluate the proposal: *Strengths* (S), *Weaknesses* (W), *Opportunities* (O), *and Threats* (T). Strengths and

weaknesses pertain to the internal resources your organization has that help implement the proposals. Opportunities and threats apply to issues external to the organization.

6. Have each group begin with a discussion of the *strengths* their organization brings to the proposal under review. Look at such things as:

   - expertise

   - motivation

   - financial resources

   - physical resources and facilities

   - reputation

   - strategic direction

   - efficiency

7. Continue with a discussion of the *weaknesses* the organization brings to the proposal under review. Point out that *weaknesses* can be overcome.

8. Next, ask the groups to discuss the *opportunities* before them, that is, the favorable conditions that exist *outside* of the organization that they can take advantage of.

9. Finally, discuss the *threats* or obstacles facing them, over and above the ones they have direct control over. These represent the hurdles they must cope with, even if they cannot completely overcome them.

10. Having explored a proposal from these vantage points, encourage the group to come to conclusions about their proposal.

11. Invite each group to present its proposal and the analysis.

# Other Options

1. Ask participants to come to the session with one change they would like to see in their organization. Place participants into small groups and invite each participant to share that wish. Allow time for interested

participants to obtain advice from others in their groups on how to achieve that goal.

2. Ask participants to assume they are on a long-range planning committee for their organization. What issues would they tackle? Use force-field analysis as their process. Begin by choosing an issue. Then establish "the current state of affairs" with regard to the issue. And then identify "the ideal state of affairs." List the obstacles in the way of progress. Brainstorm solutions.

# *Your Current Practices*

How do you currently do the following in your organization?

- Market your product or services

- Provide customer service

- Develop company morale

- Manage performance

- Work collaboratively

- Conduct strategic planning

- Seek and manage talent

# 11 TEACHING AND COACHING EMPLOYEES

# 50 Making Butterflies: It's Not What You Say That Counts

## Introductory Remarks

In this exercise, participants are asked to make butterflies from sheets of paper. Because the facilitator does not allow questions after a scripted set of unclear directions, the outcome is hilarious. A roomful of different creations demonstrates how easily giving poor verbal directions leads to a variety of interpretations of even the simplest ones (for example, "Fold your paper in half"). This brief exercise packs a wallop. It is based on a classic exercise about the drawbacks of one-way communication but with a few twists of my own. I use it to start off every workshop on active learning that I conduct because it always works as a fun, but compelling way to introduce the pitfalls of relying on lecturing as the best way to teach.

## *Objectives*

- To demonstrate that words can be easily misinterpreted.

- To illuminate the importance of active learner involvement.

- To introduce the idea that participants need to take some responsibility for their own learning.

**Group Size:** unlimited.

**Time Required:** 10 minutes

# *Materials*

- One copy of Directions for Making a Model Butterfly for the facilitator

- One copy of the Keys to Effective Teaching handout for each participant

- One sheet of (preferably colored) paper for each participant

- A sample butterfly made from the Directions sheet

# *Activity Flow*

1. Distribute a sheet of paper to each participant. (Using a colored sheet is better than white.)

2. Tell the participants the following: "I'm going to give you some simple directions to make a butterfly." Hold up a sample butterfly made from the instructions on the Directions for Making a Model Butterfly sheet. Display the sample butterfly so that all participants can see it. Hold up your butterfly for at least 15 seconds. Keep displaying it as you say: "You also can make a similar butterfly by listening to my simple directions. Because our time is limited, however, I will not answer any questions. Just listen carefully. I will go slowly."

3. Without comment, remove your sample butterfly from view. Proceed with the following:

   - "Pick up your sheet of paper and hold it in front of you."

   - "The first thing I want you to do is to fold your sheet of paper in half." [Give them plenty of time to do this.]

   - "Now tear off the upper right-hand corner." [Wait about 15 to 20 seconds.]

   - "Fold it in half again and tear off the upper left-hand corner of the sheet."

   - "Fold it in half again. Now tear off the lower right-hand corner of the sheet."

■ "Now open your folded paper and let's see what you have. If I did a good job of communicating, and you did a good job of listening, all of our sheets should look like butterflies."

4. Hold your sample butterfly up for them to see. Note participants whose creations qualify as butterflies. (They will be in the minority.) Observe the wide variety of creations produced by participants as a result of your inadequate directions. There will probably be much laughter. Ask the group members why their papers do not match yours exactly. You will probably get responses like "You put away your butterfly," "You didn't let us ask questions!" or "Your directions could be interpreted in different ways."

5. Acknowledge that, on purpose, you did not give clear, detailed instructions, allow questions, or continue to display the finished product as you went along. You also did not encourage participants to compare what they were doing as you gave each instruction. There were many things you could have done to be more effective.

6. Inquire whether you should have explained and demonstrated the folding and tearing step-by-step with the participants. Most participants will agree. Caution, however, that doing so would involve imitation, not real learning. Only by eventually making a butterfly without any prompts would participants ensure that the process has been internalized.

7. Here comes a surprise. There are always some participants who do make the butterfly even though your teaching was so restrictive. Ask the successful "butterfly makers" if they were just lucky that their folding and tearing turned into a butterfly. Most will claim that it was not luck. What they did was remember in their minds your initial butterfly when it was displayed and figured out how to produce one by themselves. Compliment them for *taking responsibility for their own learning*, something all learners have to do for learning to stick.

8. Reinforce the implications of the exercise by distributing the Keys to Effective Teaching handout.

# Other Options

1. Change the exercise to the classic version about the pitfalls of one-way communication. Distribute a sheet of paper to each participant. (Using a colored sheet is better than white.) Conduct the same exercise except this time ask each participant to close his or her eyes throughout the giving of directions. Explain that you will follow the same instructions as they do, but with your eyes open.

   It does not matter what you create. Just follow the directions as you see fit. After the third fold and tear-off, invite participants to open their eyes and unfold their sheets. You do the same. Display your creation (whatever it turns out to be). Ask: "Did I do a good job of explaining what I did?" Participants will laugh. You can then have them figure out why there was a wide variety of outcomes in the group and what can be learned from the experience.

2. Ask participants to suggest words that are open to different interpretations because the context is not clear. A good starting point is the word *run,* which has multiple meanings.

# *Directions for Making a Model Butterfly*

MAKE THE BUTTERFLY from the same type of 8.5 by 11–inch paper you will distribute to participants. Holding the paper vertically, fold it in half, downwards, and tear off the upper-right-hand corner. Next, fold the paper again toward your right, so that the top corner aligns with the torn corner. Tear off the overlapping corner. Fold the paper downward so that the bottom right corner aligns with the two previously torn corners. Tear off the overlapping piece, so that you are holding a folded paper with the bottom-right-hand corner completely torn off. When you unfold the paper, you will have a butterfly.

The trick to making the butterfly is to tear off (initially) the upper-right-hand corner and then rotate that paper so that each subsequent tear occurs in the same corner as the previous tear. Also, your first fold will be from top to bottom, not from side to side, as some participants will do. The completed butterfly has the shape shown below.

Be sure to prepare your butterfly ahead of time so that participants cannot watch you do it.

# *Keys to Effective Teaching*

1. Use clear words with just enough detail to promote understanding. Be easy to listen to by avoiding jargon and employing examples and analogies that are participant-friendly.

2. Add visuals to reinforce your words. Use presentation slides, props, and demonstrations to assist participants.

3. Encourage questions. You might decide to accomplish this by having participants work in pairs to create questions or ask them to write out questions on cards.

4. Provide ample opportunity not only for teacher-participant interaction but also for peer discussion. Use pairs, trios, or table groups for this purpose.

5. Enhance your teaching by inviting participants to do an activity related to your topic. Allow participants to perform skills without too much guidance so that they become confident that they can do them on their own.

6. Look for opportunities for participants to explain ideas and teach information and skills to each other.

**Brain-Friendly Teaching: Using Four Key Principles**

---

**Introductory Remarks**

Your participants' brains are your best allies. Too often, trainers think that there is nothing going on in their participants' heads. Nothing could be further from the truth. Your task is two-fold: to interest their brains in what you are presenting and to help their brains to really go to work so that they learn from and retain the presentation as well. Four key principles are used in the following activity to enable your teaching and coaching efforts to be brain-friendly.

---

## Objectives

- To experience teaching that is not brain-friendly.

- To use four key principles to infuse brain-friendliness into teaching.

**Group Size:** a minimum of eight

**Time Required:** 40 minutes

## Materials

- One copy of the Ways to Be a More Brain-Friendly Teacher handout for each participant

- One copy of the Your Plan handout for each participant

# *Activity Flow*

1. Select some factual or conceptual information that can be presented in a 10-minute presentation. Here are some suggestions:

   - The Situational Leadership Model

   - Characteristics of Effective Teams

   - Key Facts About Adult Learning

   - Legal Guidelines in Establishing a Case of Sexual Harassment

   - Guidelines for Videoconferencing

2. Present the information in a clear, straightforward manner. Be enthusiastic. However, lessen the effectiveness of your teaching by doing the following:

   - Plunge right into the subject matter without building interest first.

   - Fail to provide examples, analogies, and visuals.

   - Talk without interruption.

   - End without reinforcing what's been presented.

3. When your teaching is complete, have the participants count off by 4's and assign each participant one of the four ways to improve the brain-friendliness of your teaching described in the Ways to Be a More Brain-Friendly Teacher handout (for example, the "1"s get building interest, the "2"s maximizing understanding and retention, the "3"s involving participants during teaching, and the "4"s reinforcing what is taught). Ask the participants to work individually to come up with some suggestions related to their assigned areas that would have improved your teaching.

4. Create pairs or quartets of participants with the same assignment. Ask them to share their suggestions with one another.

5. Create new quartets that include one person from each of the four areas. Ask them to report to each other the suggestions each had for the category assigned to them.

6. Reconvene the total group and elicit overall suggestions.

7. Reinforce the experience by explaining that good teachers know how to connect with the brains of their participants. They assume that learners bring brainpower to the class and know how to channel it to what is being learned.

8. Ask the participants to form new pairs and to compose a question or comment about any of the suggestions made on the handout.

9. Hold a "press conference" in which you field questions from the participants. To make it more fun, ask the participants to identify the media sources they represent (for example, "I am Cindy from CNN").

10. Invite participants to complete the Your Plan handout. Encourage participants to share their ideas with each other.

# Other Options

1. If time is available, allow participants to actually conduct their brain-friendly presentations (their improvements on your presentation) and obtain peer feedback. To provide every participant with this opportunity, create small groups that meet in a relatively private place and in which each member takes a turn teaching. Encourage group members to give feedback and suggestions based on the worksheet categories.

2. Invite one or two volunteers to conduct a brain-friendly lecture for the entire group. Facilitate feedback from participants.

# *Ways to Be a More Brain-Friendly Teacher*

**Building Interest**

1. *Lead-Off Story or Interesting Visual:* Provide a relevant anecdote, fictional story, cartoon, or graphic that captures the audience's attention to what you are about to teach.

2. *Initial Case Problem:* Present a problem around which the lecture will be structured.

3. *Test Question:* Ask participants a question (even if they have little prior knowledge) so that they will be motivated to listen to your lecture for the answer.

**Maximizing Understanding and Retention**

4. *Headlines:* Reduce the major points in the lecture and in handouts to key words that act as verbal subheadings or memory aids.

5. *Examples and Analogies:* Provide real-life illustrations of the ideas in the lecture and, if possible, create a comparison between your material and the knowledge/experience the participants already have.

6. *Visual Backup:* Use flip charts, transparencies, brief handouts, and demonstrations that enable participants to see as well as hear what you are saying.

**Involving Participants During the Lecture**

7. *Spot Challenges:* Interrupt the lecture periodically and challenge participants to give examples of the concepts presented thus far or answer spot quiz questions.

8. *Illuminating Exercises:* Throughout the presentation, intersperse brief activities that illuminate the points you are making.

## Reinforcing the Lecture

9. *Application Problem:* Pose a problem or question for participants to solve based on the information given in the lecture.

10. *Participant Review:* Ask participants to review the contents of the lecture with each other or give them a self-scoring review test.

# *Your Plan*

List below ideas on how you might increase the brain-friendliness of your teaching of a concept, model, or procedure. Think of ideas such as:

- Lead-off story
- Opening visual
- Test question
- Headlines
- Examples and analogies
- Visuals (besides slides)

# 52 Building Skills Through Role Plays: You Have Options

───────── **Introductory Remarks** ─────────

Asking a trainer to avoid role playing is like asking a
carpenter to avoid using a hammer. Role playing is vital
to the practice of skills. When participants are resistant to
it, a trainer has to find ways to overcome this resistance.
In this activity, participants learn that there are many role-
playing options and build their toolkits of strategies.

## Objectives

- To determine why role playing is often resisted.
- To use a menu of role-playing options to increase the possible "best choices" for different situations.

**Group Size:** at least six participants

**Time Required:** 30 minutes

## Materials

- One copy of the Options in Role Playing handout for each participant

## Activity Flow

1. Mention that after specific skills are demonstrated, it is important to practice them together in order to build confidence in conducting the entire skill set. This is best accomplished through the use of role play.

2. Ask participants to suggest reasons why trainees may not like to role play.

3. Compare their responses to the following list:

   ■ Role playing might make participants anxious and uncomfortable.

   ■ Role playing might feel artificial or contrived to participants.

   ■ Participants feel judged and singled out.

   ■ Group feedback to role playing is negative and unsupportive.

   ■ Role playing deteriorates into play; participants are not serious.

   ■ Those not participating are passive and bored.

4. Point out that when role playing produces negative feelings, the purpose of role playing—*to enable trainees to experiment with new behaviors in a safe setting and receive constructive feedback*—is defeated. People are not apt to be open to learning when they feel incompetent, defensive, artificial, silly, or bored.

5. Ask participants to suggest ways to introduce and facilitate role playing so that its purpose is achieved.

6. Explain that role playing is often conducted in only one way, that is, a participant is called on to perform in front of the entire training group, who then critique the participant's performance. Indicate that there are a number of other choices about how to design role-playing practice.

7. Form trios and distribute the Options in Role Playing handout to participants. Assign one member of each trio to read each section of the handout.

8. Ask each trio member to summarize the information assigned to him or her and share that summary with the other two members of the trio.

9. Reconvene the whole group and ask participants whether they have any questions about the material they have read. If there are no questions, pose these questions back to participants:

   ■ Which role-playing options would make participants less anxious than others? (possible answers: breaking into small groups, reading prepared scripts, rotating roles quickly so that participants do not have to perform for a long period of time)

- How can you make a role play as realistic as possible? (answer: set up a role play scene that is based on an actual experience of one of the participants)

- What is a way to design role playing that combines practice and immediate feedback? (answer: adding one or more observers to a role-playing group)

## Other Options

1. Give participants a variety of situations and ask them to choose those options from the handout that best match the situations.

2. Obtain volunteers to facilitate role-playing situations. Invite them to try out one or more role-playing methods. Obtain feedback from the entire group.

# *Options in Role Playing*

## *Scripting*

Scripting is concerned with the development of roles and the situation in which the drama is placed. Here are six options:

1. *Improvisation.* Participants can be given a general scenario and asked to fill in the details themselves. This approach promotes spontaneity and the opportunity to gear the scenario to one's own work experience. Because the situation is not clearly outlined, however, participants may have difficulty creating details on their own.

2. *Prescribed roles.* Participants can be given a well-prepared set of instructions that state the facts about the roles they are portraying and how they are to behave. This approach gives you the most control over the script, so the dramatic tension you want to create is easily obtainable. However, participants may not identify with the roles and situation you have developed or they may get lost if the scenario is too complex.

3. *Semi-prescribed roles.* Participants can be given information about the situation and the characters to be portrayed but not told how to handle the situation. By not prescribing how characters are to behave, this approach provides greater latitude for the participants. Some of them, however, may create a scenario different from what the trainer intended.

4. *Replay of life.* Participants can portray themselves in situations they have actually faced. This approach has the advantage of bringing the most realism to the drama. However, it can be difficult to re-create the actual situation and the role play may then flounder.

5. *Participant-prepared skits.* Participants can be asked to develop a role-playing vignette of their own. This approach provides them with time to create a role play and gives them a chance to rehearse before a final performance. Participants will respond especially well to this approach if they are invited to address their real-life problems and to incorporate them into the skits. However, some of the spontaneity of the previous options is lost.

6. *Dramatic readings.* Participants can be given a previously prepared script to act out. This approach creates the least anxiety of any of the previous options and allows the least skill practice.

# *Staging*

Staging is concerned with the format you use for the role play, regardless of the content. Here are six options.

1. *Informal role playing.* The role play can evolve informally from a group discussion. An informal format reduces the stage fright often experienced with role playing.

2. *Stage-front role playing.* One pair, trio, or the like can role play in front of the group, which will observe and offer feedback. Staging a stage-front group role play focuses the class on a single drama for later discussion and feedback and allows for maximum coaching and feedback by the trainer. Often, stage-front role plays are the most anxiety-producing for the participants chosen. In addition, the rest of the participants are relegated to observer roles.

3. *Simultaneous role playing.* All participants can be formed into pairs for a two-person drama, trios for a three-person drama, and so on and simultaneously undertake their role plays. A multiple-group format reduces anxiety and allows everyone to participate. However, the trainer may have difficulty monitoring the dramas that unfold and the level of performance demonstrated by participants.

4. *Rotational role playing.* Actors in front of the group can be rotated, usually by interrupting the role play in progress and replacing one or more of the actors. Although this option involves a single-group drama, several participants can still be included. This approach is less demanding than a non-rotating stage-front drama.

5. *Use of different actors.* More than one actor can be recruited to role play the same situation in its entirety. This allows the group to observe more than one style or approach. The trainer has to be careful, however, not to

encourage comparisons between the actors that would lessen somebody's self-esteem. Also, obtaining volunteers to be the actors can be difficult.

6. *Repeated role playing.* Regardless of the staging option chosen, the role play can be reenacted. This is always a good idea when you want participants to have a second chance after the initial feedback.

# *Processing*

A final set of six choices has to do with *processing* the role play. Processing pertains to reflective discussion or debriefing of the role play or to giving performance feedback to the role players.

1. *Designated observers.* One or more observers can be added to each role-playing group and given specific instructions about what to observe and how to give feedback. (If you are using a single, stage-front role play, choose specific participants to be feedback observers.) Peer feedback is a two-edged sword. Participants are less threatened by it but, at the same time, they may not value it as much as the trainer's feedback.

2. *Self-assessment.* The role players themselves can discuss their reactions to the experience. Ask open-ended questions first so that the role players are free to make observations on their own. Ask more pointed questions later on, probing gently about feelings, intentions, and reactions.

3. *Open audience discussion and feedback.* Invite the group as a whole to give their reactions and feedback to a role play. You can avoid a free-for-all feedback session by providing guidelines such as asking the audience to give positive feedback first or to focus on specific events rather than global impressions. Try to obtain several points of view because different observers notice different things.

4. *Subgroup discussion and feedback.* Assign a small group from the audience to each one of the role players and ask the members to discuss what they saw happening. This technique is especially effective after the format of

use of different actors. Ask the subgroup members to use the time not only to give feedback but also to obtain the actor's self-assessment.

5. *Trainer observations.* You can give your reactions to the role play for everyone to hear. Because your feedback is often held in high regard, be careful to preserve the self-esteem of the role players and "own" the feedback by saying such phrases as "It seemed to me . . ." or "I'm not sure how others saw this, but I. . . ."

6. *Benchmark comparison.* The role players and observers can compare the performance to an ideal script. Be sure, however, to give participants the opportunity to disagree with the "ideal."

## **53** **The Components of Effective Coaching: Observing the Process**

### Introductory Remarks

Here is a well-known activity based on a drawing of a young girl/old woman originally published in *Puck* in 1915 as "My Wife and My Mother-in-Law." This multiple picture has often been used to examine stereotyping and group pressure on perception. Typically, participants are asked to relate their feelings and opinions about the woman they see in the drawing, not realizing that the drawing can be viewed in two different ways. Instead, you can use this drawing as the basis for an interesting coaching exercise.

## *Objectives*

- To observe how we typically approach coaching.
- To identify the components of effective coaching.

**Group Size:** any

**Time Required:** 15 to 20 minutes

## *Materials*

- A copy of "My Wife and My Mother-in-Law" (You can obtain this drawing by googling "My Wife and My Mother-in-Law") for the coachee

## *Activity Flow*

1. Obtain two volunteers. One is to be a coach. He or she should be a person who has previously seen the drawing. (There are always some participants who have!) The other volunteer is to be a person who needs assistance in seeing both women. If there are no such volunteers, perform the role yourself, pretending that you can only see the "old woman."

2. The volunteer coach should try to show the other person how to "see" both women. As this goes on, ask the remaining participants to focus on how the volunteer coaches.

3. After the coachee has been helped to see both women, observers should tell the coach in as descriptive terms as possible what he or she did in assisting the other person.

4. Discuss what behaviors were helpful or harmful in loosening up the person's perceptions of the drawing. Compare these behaviors to common coaching situations. For example, if the coach failed to ask the coachee which woman he or she saw, note that it is often helpful "to begin with the learner," that is, the coach should first focus on what the coachee understands before giving his or her own guidance.

5. Indicate that there is no one right way to go about coaching. Point out, however, that the following components of effective coaching apply in many situations:

   - *Assess* first what the employee knows or how he or she sees the task or procedure.

   - *Show and explain* how you want the task or procedure to be done. (For visual learners, show first; for auditory learners, explain first. If it is a complex task, give an overview first. Break up the demonstration and explanation into small parts.)

   - Ask the employee to *perform* the task and/or *state* his or her understanding of the assignment so that you can give feedback.

- *Evaluate* at a later point the employee's performance. Be available for questions and further assistance.

6. Demonstrate the steps above, preferably using one of the coaching situations identified in your training program.


## Other Options ────────────────

1. Choose any reasonably difficult skill that one person can coach another to do (knitting, yo-yo, using sign-language).

2. Have participants discuss how they like to be coached. Use these questions:

   - Do you prefer to watch something thoroughly demonstrated before doing it yourself?

   - Do you like a lot of verbal explanation? Use of a manual?

   - Do you like to try something new yourself first?

   - Do you prefer step-by-step instruction?

   - Do you want to know *why* you are asked to do something as much as *what* you are to do?

## 54  Show But Not Tell: Upping the Stakes

**———— Introductory Remarks ————**

Learning is not a matter of monkey see, monkey do. Many
teachers and coaches make the mistake of prompting
the learner rather than challenging him or her. By that,
I mean that they encourage learning by imitation and
repetition rather than encouraging the learner to take a
more active role. This activity drives this point home.

## Objectives

- To demonstrate an active learning way to teach a skill.
- To practice the "show but not tell" technique.

**Group Size:** any

**Time Required:** 20 to 30 minutes

## Materials

- One copy of the Show But Not Tell in One-to-One Coaching handout
  for each participant

## Activity Flow

1. Decide on a multi-step procedure you want participants to learn. You
   might choose any of the following:

   - Using a computer application

- Filling out an office requisition form

- Operating machinery

- Taking applications from customers

- Performing any work-related action that involves physical effort

2. Ask the participants to watch you perform the entire procedure. Just do it, with little or no explanation or commentary about what and why you are doing what you do. (Telling the participants what you are doing will lessen their mental alertness.) Give the participants a visual glimpse of the "big picture" of the entire job. Do not expect retention. At this point, you are merely establishing readiness for learning.

3. Form the participants into pairs. Demonstrate the first part of the procedure again, with little or no explanation or commentary. *Ask pairs to discuss with each other what they observed you doing.* Obtain a volunteer to explain what you did. If the participants have difficulty following the procedure, demonstrate again. Acknowledge correct observations.

4. Have the pairs practice with each other the first part of the procedure. When it is mastered, proceed with a silent demonstration of the remaining parts of the procedure, following each part with paired practice.

5. Have the participants do the procedure by themselves without any guidance.

6. Distribute the Show But Not Tell handout. Explain that it contains instructions to use this technique in one-to-one coaching situations.

# Other Options

1. If possible, ask participants to attempt a procedure before any demonstration. Encourage guesses and an openness to making mistakes. By doing this, you will immediately get participants mentally involved. Then have them watch you demonstrate.

2. If some participants master the procedure sooner than others, recruit them as "silent demonstrators" to practice the method of "show, but not tell" themselves.

# *Show But Not Tell in One-to-One Coaching*

Here are four steps to use this technique:

## *1. Observe*

Ask the learner to watch you perform the skill. Just do it, with little or no explanation or commentary about what you are doing. Give the learner a visual glimpse of the "big picture." Do not expect retention. At this point, you are merely establishing readiness for learning and providing an overview.

## *2. Recall*

Demonstrate the skill slowly again, with little or no explanation or commentary. Ask the learner what he or she observed you doing. Acknowledge correct observations.

## *3. Question*

Ask for questions. Because the learner has been actively involved in the process of observing the skill, he or she will have more questions than if you had taught the skill in a traditional manner.

## *4. Do*

Have the learner try to do the skill "to test yourself." Encourage him or her to practice until he or she is confident that the skill has been mastered.

# 12 UNDERSTANDING OTHERS ——————

#  Avoiding Labels: Interpreting Behavior Objectively

## Introductory Remarks

In this exercise, participants learn about Steve, a difficult
co-worker, from the point of view of one of his colleagues.
Participants are then asked to describe someone in their
workplace whose behavior is also mystifying. Both descriptions
tend to "label" the difficult co-worker rather than try
to understand him or her. From this discovery, participants
experience how easily we interpret the behavior of
others by labels and how we can seek a better
understanding.

## *Objectives*

- To confront how we use labels to interpret someone's behaviors.

- To recognize ways to interpret behavior that are non-evaluative and
  open to further examination.

**Group Size:** any size.

**Time Required:** 40 minutes

## *Materials*

- One copy of the Interpreting Behavior handout for each participant
- One copy of the Rethinking Helen handout for each participant

# *Activity Flow*

1. Distribute the Interpreting Behavior handout.

2. Request that someone read aloud the description of Steve on this handout.

3. Ask participants whether they have met someone like Steve. Obtain responses.

4. Ask each participant to choose a person who puzzles him or her and write why in the space provided on the handout. The choice does not have to be a person who is really annoying. It could be someone who's too quiet and hard to read, or perhaps a manager who's much more formal than most people in your organization. Allow 5 minutes for this process.

5. Explain that one of the problems we often have in understanding people is our tendency to write them off when their behavior doesn't make sense to us.

6. Refer participants to the description of Steve as a case in point. Ask participants to notice how Steve's co-worker describes him as you read the description a second time. Obtain examples of labeling (such as "arrogant").

7. Explain that many people function like Steve's co-worker. When they don't "get" someone, they often interpret the person's behavior subjectively. They put the person "in a box," just like Steve's co-worker did. But that doesn't help.

8. State that we may be most likely to label people when we are out of our comfort zones. This can happen when they are very different from us in values, style, and preferences. We keep our distance and reconfirm our labels. Sometimes the labeling occurs because the other person is like us in ways we would hate to admit to ourselves. Often we even go beyond labeling to attributing motives that have no basis in fact. When we misinterpret or distort who the person is, it doesn't help us understand him or her.

9. Instruct participants to go back and reread their own descriptions of difficult persons. Did they label the person in some way? Say that the better way is to keep one's judgments in check and try to develop a more objective understanding of a person whose behavior is puzzling or even negative. One may not like or accept the other person's behavior, but can still be less evaluative and be open to understanding how and why the person acts in the ways he or she does. Trying to be understanding does not mean that you are excusing the person's actions.

10. Explain that there are many benefits to being "curious, not furious." Distribute the Rethinking Helen handout as an example. After reading about this co-worker rethinking her interpretation of Helen, ask participants to return to their first interpretations of a difficult person to understand and share with partners how they might rethink their initial judgments.

11. End by asking participants: "What are you taking away from this activity?"


## Other Options

1. Ask the group to nominate a well-known person, alive or dead, whose behavior is puzzling. It can be someone whose behavior is loathsome (for example, Bernard Madoff) or just odd (for example, George Castanza of "Seinfeld" fame). Use the same directions as above, substituting that person for someone they personally know.

2. For a faster way to explore the themes of the above activity, use a word-association game. It will not have quite the same experiential impact, but it still works. Identify an attribute that may be perceived in different ways, such as "moody." Ask participants to call out words they associate with this attribute. List responses. Then have participants examine the list, noting words that are subjective rather than objective. For example, "lazy" is subjective, while "does not do more than is required" is more objective. Tie in this experience with some of the major points raised above.

# *Interpreting Behavior*

Steve is arrogant, opinionated, and sloppy about his work . . . yet highly critical of others. He often makes crude or insensitive comments to people and reacts very defensively to any type of suggestion or criticism, no matter how constructive.

Steve "stumbled" onto his job at our company. Despite the training he's received, the job is a little out of his league. He knows it. And he knows that everyone else knows it. Yet he gives off an air of superiority. He won't ask for help or advice. And if help or advice is offered, he rejects it.

I JUST DON'T GET HIM.

Describe below someone you just don't get.

_____

_____

_____

_____

_____

_____

_____

_____

_____

_____

_____

_____

_____

# *Rethinking Helen*

In the accounting office where I work as office manager, Helen is an accountant. We are as different from each other as possible and I clash with her often. I confess that I've made very little effort to understand her values, assumptions, and motivation. We're different in many ways. Helen seems unhappy all the time. She often grunts and grumbles under her breath, resists getting excited about anything, and doesn't respond to jokes or attempts by others to generate good cheer. She seems to hold back. I, on the other hand, try to create a positive atmosphere with co-workers through cheerful greetings and friendly comments throughout the day. Helen just focuses on her work and keeps reminding everyone of the overwhelming responsibility she has. She tries to boss or bully others into doing her work and blames others when problems arise. She eats lunch at her desk and never joins others in the lunchroom or comes to work-related social events. I try to do my work without complaint, help others, and contribute to a pleasant work environment. Helen is a single mother, living with her elderly parents in their home, and both of her parents have had some serious health problems in recent years. I am married and live with my husband and two of my three young adult daughters in my own home.

　　Which of these differences may be hindering my ability to understand Helen? Looking at the world through her eyes, I can see that she is overwhelmed with responsibility. From raising her child alone, to taking care of her parents and then coming to work to order other people's financial lives—many of whom make a lot more money than she does—I can see how she might feel like the world is against her. I can also see that being cheerful and having a sense of humor may be beyond her reach right now. Maybe she feels that others in the office have more advantages than she and take our good fortune for granted. Perhaps Helen is more in a survival mode, just getting through the days and not able to think beyond to future goals, career issues, retirement, and such. It must be frightening to face the responsibilities she has alone, with no one to share her feelings with. Maybe she withdraws because she cannot identify with the rest of us. I have a long way to go before I understand her, but at least I recognize my own complacency—and I want to change that.

# 56 Be Curious, Not Furious: Five Ways to Understand Others

## Introductory Remarks

In this activity, participants assess how much effort they have given to trying to understand the puzzling behaviors of other people. *A warning*: You may have to push people to be honest with themselves. Few people engage in these suggested behaviors on a regular basis. Saying to themselves, "I've done that," may signify that the action was taken only once.

## *Objectives*

- To enlarge the possibilities of how to understand other people.
- To apply the five ways to a person a participant finds difficult.

**Group Size:** at least six
**Time Required:** 30 minutes

## *Materials*

- One copy of the Five Tips for Understanding Others handout for each participant

## *Activity Flow*

1. When faced with difficult people, we typically have one or more of three responses:
    - We may avoid them whenever possible.

- We may complain about them to a trusted colleague.

- We may give them back a dose of their own medicine.

2. Ask participants whether they have reacted to difficult people in any of these ways. Then ask: "Did reacting that way improve your relationship?" Make the point: "When we give up on a difficult person, our relationship remains at an impasse. But if we can get ourselves *curious* about *why* the person acts as he does, rather than just be *furious* about *what* he does, we may find that three things can happen:

   - We may gain a perspective that helps us avoid taking the challenger's behavior too personally.

   - We may unlock new ways to relate to the person that will be more productive.

   - We may win some appreciation from the person that can serve as the basis for a better relationship.

3. Distribute the Five Tips handout. Ask participants to study the handout with partners and to identify the suggestions that most need to be used more effectively in their own lives.

4. Next, have them share some background about a person each finds difficult at the current time. (The challenging aspects of that person may be just a few or several.) Ask participants to find tips from the handout that they can use in a renewed effort at understanding the difficult person.

5. Reconvene the entire group. Ask participants what they are taking away from this activity.

## Other Options

1. Discuss the five tips and rank order those with the most potential for improving the participants' difficult relationships. Either use a poll or build a group consensus.

2. Have participants establish an action plan, the goal of which is to increase their understanding of difficult people they know.

# *Five Tips for Understanding Others*

1. *Take time to listen to the person.* When a challenging person talks, give him or her your full attention, without "running your own tape" about what you'll say next. Try to avoid interrupting or simply tuning the person out. You might even paraphrase what you hear the person saying, so that he or she gets the idea that you're really listening.

2. *Ask questions about his or her thoughts and feelings.* Use open-ended questions to draw out new information and clarify what you are hearing. This is especially important when you want to understand a relatively taciturn individual who keeps a lot inside. Open-ended questions invite the speaker to expand or elaborate on her message.

3. *Consult other people who may have insights about this person.* Who seems to have more success with this person? Ask for that person's perspective about your challenger and for suggestions on new approaches to try. Even if you find that everyone you know has the same feelings about this person as you do, others may have different ways of coping.

4. *"Walk in his or her shoes" by looking at events from this person's point of view.* Imagine you *are* the other person and ask yourself how a specific situation would look to you, what you'd be feeling, and what your concerns might be. This is not an easy task. It's hard to put aside how you would look at the situation. Recognize that the other person may look at things differently than you do.

5. *Try out some new ways to relate to the person.* Identify how you typically "dance" with the person. Are you avoiding? Critical? Forgiving? Demanding? Be curious enough to see what would happen if you act in a dramatically

different way. For example, you might consider one of
the following new behaviors:

- Take extra time to build rapport and establish trust.

- Be firmer and more consistent about what you expect.

- Take a positive approach by reinforcing and encouraging this
  person.

- Ask this person to tell you about his or her views, needs, and
  concerns.

- Back off on a big change; focus on little ones.

- Be more honest and straight about what you think and feel.

- Be more persistent with your efforts to influence this person. Don't
  let up.

**Comparing Yourself to Others: Looking for Differences and Similarities**

---
## Introductory Remarks
---

In this activity, participants assess themselves in comparison with others. This is a useful action, since it stands to reason that comparing yourself to another person helps you to gain lots of insight into the relationship. Instead of choosing just one indicator, I have found it useful to make the comparison on a number of fronts (interpersonal style, gender, age, and culture). Note how the following activity achieves this result in one fell swoop.

## *Objectives*

- To compare yourself to someone else as a window to mutual understanding.
- To identify similarities and differences between two people in a work or personal relationship.

**Group Size:** at least six
**Time Required:** 30 minutes

## *Materials*

- One copy of the Comparing Yourself to Someone Else handout for each participant

## *Activity Flow*

1. Explain that the more we can recognize the glasses others see the world through, the better we can understand their perspectives and behavior. This is especially true if we compare how their glasses may differ from or agree with our own.

2. Distribute the Comparing Yourself to Someone Else handout and carefully go over the directions.

3. Invite participants to complete the handout and explain to partners the similarities and differences between themselves and the other persons they have chosen.

4. Reconvene the entire group. Ask some of the following questions:

   - On average, were you very different from the other person? Do you need to put more effort into "walking in his or her shoes"?

   - On average, were you very similar to the other person? If so, do you like what you see?

   - How can being similar to and also different from another person be possible?

## Other Options

1. Poll participants about the category in which there was the greatest difference. Similarity? What conclusions can you draw from this?

2. If participants know each other, invite them to compare how they saw themselves.

# *Comparing Yourself to Someone Else*

*Instructions:* Select a person with whom you have difficulties from time to time. Circle the point on each continuum that fits the way you see that person. Put a square on the point that fits the way you see yourself.

Spontaneous . . . . . . . . . . . . . . . . . . . . . . . . . . . . Deliberate

Social . . . . . . . . . . . . . . . . . . . . . . . . . . . . . . . . . Private

Emotional . . . . . . . . . . . . . . . . . . . . . . . . . . . . . Logical

Take-charge . . . . . . . . . . . . . . . . . . . . . . . . . . . . Responsive

Seek to fix things . . . . . . . . . . . . . . . . . . . . . . . . Seek to discuss things

Competitive . . . . . . . . . . . . . . . . . . . . . . . . . . . . Collaborative

Seek independence . . . . . . . . . . . . . . . . . . . . . . . Seek relationships

Give opinions . . . . . . . . . . . . . . . . . . . . . . . . . . . Ask questions

Intense . . . . . . . . . . . . . . . . . . . . . . . . . . . . . . . . Easygoing

Need to focus . . . . . . . . . . . . . . . . . . . . . . . . . . . Collaborative

Loyal . . . . . . . . . . . . . . . . . . . . . . . . . . . . . . . . . . Uncommitted

Need to control others . . . . . . . . . . . . . . . . . . . . Need to control self

Confronting . . . . . . . . . . . . . . . . . . . . . . . . . . . . Avoiding

Self-oriented . . . . . . . . . . . . . . . . . . . . . . . . . . . . Group-oriented

Respect for talent . . . . . . . . . . . . . . . . . . . . . . . . Respect for authority

Loose . . . . . . . . . . . . . . . . . . . . . . . . . . . . . . . . . Rule-oriented

# 58 The Three C's: What Makes People Difficult

## Introductory Remarks

This activity helps each participant to reframe his or her understanding of another person. By seeing that difficult behavior is often connected to an underlying anxiety, participants have the opportunity to rethink their understanding of others. I have found that this notion shakes people up a bit. Rather than focusing on their own reactions to the person, participants come to grips with another choice—what the person in question is experiencing.

## *Objectives*

- To reveal some underlying reasons for people's difficult behavior.
- To assess new ways of responding to a difficult person.

**Group Size:** any

**Time Required:** 30 minutes

## *Materials*

- One copy of Sources of Anxiety for each participant
- One copy of Working the Three C's for each participant

## *Activity Flow*

1. Explain that one tool for understanding difficult people is to identify what the other person may be anxious about. Say that all people have been shown to have three basic needs, all beginning with the letter C:

    ■ *Control*—having power over our lives, being in the driver's seat

    ■ *Connection*—belonging, being supported, loved, accepted

    ■ *Competence*—being successful, demonstrating mastery and being recognized for it

2. Explain further that when a person is anxious about one or more needs being met, his or her behavior may be challenging to others.

3. Distribute the Sources of Anxiety handout. Ask participants to select someone they consider challenging and complete the handout with that person in mind.

4. Pair up participants and ask the pairs to share their analyses.

5. Distribute the Working the Three C's handout and ask each participant to review the handout with the person he or she identified in mind.

6. Reconvene the entire group. Debrief the analysis they just did. Ask what, if anything, wasn't clear. Did the analysis help them to understand the person better? Discuss ways in which the handout can be helpful to them in dealing with difficult people.

## Other Options

1. Have participants assess their own anxiety levels with regard to the Three C's. How do their own anxieties trigger challenging behavior from others?

2. Discuss the effect of looking at a difficult person as an anxious person. Does it mean that one should tolerate their difficult behaviors if those behaviors can be traced to anxiety about one of the Three C's?

# *Sources of Anxiety*

*How anxious is this person about meeting the following needs?*

Check any of the anxious behaviors he or she tends to exhibit:

**Control**

☐ Micromanages others

☐ Acts helpless and dependent

☐ Has great difficulty being flexible

**Connection**

☐ Rejects others

☐ Tries too hard to be accepted

☐ Seeks a lot of attention

**Competence**

☐ Brags a lot

☐ Puts him- or herself down

☐ Easily becomes defensive

# *Working the Three C's*

Below are some strategies that may help alleviate people's anxieties about *control, connection,* and *competence*. Check any that you think might be helpful for you to try with your difficult person.

**Control**

- Keep the person informed and up-to-date.

- Offer choices and decisions.

- Ask: "What role do you want [in this project]?"

**Connection**

- Show the person attention before he or she seeks it.

- Tactfully and directly set limits when he or she demands too much attention.

- Offer greetings or conversation in small doses.

**Competence**

- Give genuine positive feedback proactively.

- Don't put the person on the spot in front of others.

- Give the person a task you know he or she can do successfully.

# 13 Sales and Customer Service

## 59 | A Convincing Sales Presentation: Warm-up Practice

---
### Introductory Remarks
---

This activity is useful as a warm-up to more challenging training on effective sales presentations. Participants get to experience and receive feedback in a safe small group environment. I have used this activity often to get participants used to practicing making sales presentations before fine-tuning their skills.

---

## *Objectives*

- To experience putting together a simple presentation.
- To obtain initial feedback on one's selling skills.

**Group Size:** any

**Time Required:** 45 minutes

## *Materials*

- One copy of the A Convincing Presentation handout for each participant

## *Activity Flow*

1. Ask participants, "When giving a sales presentation, what should you do to make it convincing?" Invite responses. If not stated, include any of the following suggestions:

- Know your customers. Find out their prior exposure to the item being presented.

- Focus on how the item will benefit them.

- Use supporting facts but give just enough detail to help sway customers.

- Pause enough to allow customers to ask questions.

- Surface any concerns or objections about what you are selling.

2. Explain that the exercise to follow will give them an early opportunity to practice and obtain feedback on giving a convincing sales presentation.

3. Distribute the Convincing Presentation handout. Ask participants to complete it. Give them 5 minutes.

4. Create trios. One person will play the role of a salesperson while the other two will play the persons to be convinced. Roles will be rotated so that each person has a turn doing a presentation. Allocate about 5 minutes for each presentation.

5. After each role play, the two participants who were role playing the persons to be convinced will provide brief feedback: "What did the presenter do to be effective? What suggestions do you have to enhance the presentation?"

6. When each trio is finished, request two volunteers who would be willing to redo their presentation for the entire group.

7. After each role play, invite the group to give brief feedback.

# Other Options

1. Focus on sales presentations to larger audiences by inviting participants to present to the large group a convincing sales presentation they would give in their own organizations.

2. Limit presentations to items that most people would not like or do (for example, going on a "silent" retreat).

# A Convincing Presentation

Select something from the list below that you would recommend to others. Write at the bottom of the sheet some ways to present the value of what you have selected.

- A product or service you have found beneficial
- A place to visit
- A book or movie
- An action you do that brings good health, fitness, spirituality, or income

# 60  Dissatisfied Customers: How to Win Them Over

## ─Introductory Remarks─

This activity introduces four basic steps to overcome customer dissatisfaction. By role playing, participants have the opportunity to practice these steps. Unlike many role-play exercises, participants can re-create a real situation from their experience as a customer service provider and, hopefully, experience a better result. I wish to acknowledge Dr. Kim Stott's role in the creation of this activity.

## *Objectives*

- To consider four steps to cope with an unhappy customer.
- To practice these steps in real-life situations.

**Group Size:** any
**Time Required:** 75 to 90 minutes

## *Materials*

- One copy of the Customer Service Role Play handout for each participant
- Prepared newsprint sheet or presentation slide (see Step 2)

# *Activity Flow*

1. Explain to participants that relations with some customers often "heat up" and challenge our abilities to be responsive. As customer-oriented providers, our job is to remain cool, calm, and collected, no matter how hot our customers become. Dealing with dissatisfied customers requires skill, knowledge, and grace. Tell participants that this activity is designed to help them practice strategies to deal with even the most dissatisfied customer.

2. Indicate that there are four basic service steps they can use in any challenging service situation. These include (list on newsprint):

   - *Hear the customer out*—allow the customer the opportunity to let off steam and air his or her complaints.

   - *Empathize*—put yourself in the customer's shoes. Demonstrate that you understand where he or she is coming from.

   - *Apologize* for the problem and/or the person's dissatisfaction (even if you don't agree).

   - *Take responsibility for action*—work with the customer to find a solution to the problem. Take action to ensure that the solution is realized and that the customer is satisfied with the outcome.

3. Distribute the Customer Service Role Play handout. Direct participants to draw from their own experience with a particularly difficult, dissatisfied customer to create a role-play scenario. Allow 10 minutes for scenario creation.

4. Divide participants into trios and give the following instructions:

   - Each person will have the opportunity to act out his or her role play, playing the role of service provider.

   - Trios must begin by deciding which member will enact his or her service scenario first, who will play the customer, and who will act as the observer.

   - Providers will introduce their scenarios, carefully explaining the customer role. The job of the provider is to do whatever it takes to satisfy the customer.

- The job of the customer is to challenge the provider's service skills.

- Observers will watch the role play and furnish the provider with feedback about what the provider did that was effective and any suggestions for improvement he or she might have.

- Each member will have 10 minutes to explain and enact his or her scenario.

5. Circulate during the role plays to observe interactions.

6. After 10 minutes, stop the groups and ask the customers and the observers to provide the service provider with feedback regarding his or her customer satisfaction skills. Encourage providers to share their own impressions as well. What did they feel they did particularly well and what would they like to do better? Allow 5 minutes for the feedback session, then rotate roles and begin the next role play.

7. After all the trios have completed all three role plays and received feedback (a total of 45 minutes), reconvene the large group. Share your observations with the group and poll participants for reactions to the activity. Suggested questions for debriefing include:

- Do you now feel more confident or better prepared to deal with difficult service situations? Why? Why not?

- Did anyone learn any new service strategies he or she would like to share with the group?

# Other Options

1. Hold a discussion about dealing with angry customers. Divide participants into small groups and ask them to discuss the following:

- What tactics do angry customers use?

- What can you do to keep yourself from becoming upset and unraveled?

- How can you maximize an angry customer's satisfaction?

Ask each subgroup to nominate one person to serve on a panel to discuss the previous questions.

2. Ask participants to share their best, most terrific, most satisfying customer experiences with the group. Direct them to share their stories, explaining what happened, what made it a good experience, and what the results were.

# *Customer Service Role Play*

Recall a situation in the past when, in hindsight, a customer service interaction did not go well. The situation may have involved a difficult customer, or it may have been "one of those days" for you. Briefly describe the situation below. Please describe a situation in which you were the service provider.

Your job/position in the situation was to:

_____

_____

Describe the customer you were interacting with:

_____

_____

Describe the outcome the customer expected:

_____

_____

Describe the outcome you expected:

_____

_____

What was the actual outcome?

_____

_____

What went wrong?

_____

_____

Use the space below to list any other key details not included above:

_____

_____

_____

_____

**To Consult or Not Consult: Assessing Your Selling Style**

---
## Introductory Remarks
---

This activity is intended to help new salespeople to embrace the practice of "consultative selling," a sales approach that is dedicated to helping the customer meet his or her needs and solve problems. This activity should be used to create "buy-in" to the concept before specific question-asking skills are introduced and practiced.

---

## Objectives

- To introduce the idea of "consultative selling."
- To experience the contrast between "consultative selling" and "pressured selling."

**Group Size:** any

**Suggested Time:** 45 to 60 minutes

**Materials:** none

## Activity Flow

1. Point out that "consultative selling" is a problem-solving approach. It involves helping customers improve their profits or lower their costs instead of merely persuading them to purchase products and services. In essence, it means treating *customers* like *clients*. Consultative selling is

based on the idea that everybody wins in an enduring business relationship. Gone are the days when a salesperson shows little interest in the customer's needs during the sale and little regard for customer satisfaction afterward.

2. Divide participants into groups of three to five participants and ask them to discuss this question: "Why has this shift toward consultative selling occurred?"

3. Reconvene the entire group and obtain responses from participants.

4. Explain that you would like everyone to participate in an interesting exercise that shows what happens when salespeople do not "consult" with buyers. Re-create the small discussion groups used in Step 2. Give these instructions:

   ■ Each member of your group should identify some products or services he or she finds valuable for everyday life. Examples might include Internet banking, a cleaning fluid, a kitchen gadget, an insurance plan, and so forth.

   ■ Next, each team member should determine quickly one of those products or services that others in the team are either unfamiliar with or have not as yet purchased.

   ■ Each person now gives a 1-minute "sales presentation" about that product or service. Extol the features and benefits of the chosen product/service. However, do NOT allow others to ask questions during the presentation; also, the seller cannot in any way "consult" with the "customers" about their needs. After each presentation, team members will tell the seller whether the product or service would solve any problems they face or meet any of their personal needs.

5. Allow 15 to 20 minutes for each small group to complete giving sales presentations and receiving feedback from group members.

6. Ask participants to assess the overall degree to which the products/services that were "sold" met the needs of the "customers." Chances are that this one-way form of selling sometimes missed the needs of the customers (unless the salesperson was very lucky guessing them).

7. Ask participants the following questions:

   ▪ Why would poor results follow if we fail to consult our clients about their needs? Any examples from your work?

   ▪ In what ways are a "sell-and-bill" relationship inferior to a consultative one?

## Other Options

1. Practice "consultative selling" in either of the following two situations: purchasing a car or buying a new home.

2. Have participants brainstorm the benefits of a consultative selling approach.

# 62 Your Company's Sales Philosophy: How Do You Treat Customers?

## Introductory Remarks

Most companies don't have a sales philosophy, a customer orientation that guides its practices when interacting with customers. This activity invites participants to assess how customer-focused they are and consider changes to the current way of doing things.

## *Objectives*

- To evaluate the sales philosophy of a company.
- To consider changes in a company's sales philosophy.

**Group Size:** any
**Time Required:** 30 minutes

## *Materials*

- One copy of the Our Sales Philosophy handout for each participant

## *Activity Flow*

1. Invite participants to complete the Our Sales Philosophy handout. It assesses the degree to which "everybody wins" is the operating sales philosophy in an organization.

2. Obtain reactions to the questionnaire when participants have completed it.

3. Pair up participants. Ask partners to share with each other their responses and the reasons for them.

4. Obtain one or two volunteers who will share their company's practice with regard to each of the seven actions. Allow for questions and comments from the rest of the group.

## Other Options

1. Discuss the relative importance of the seven actions. Which ones have the highest priority in your business?

2. Brainstorm the obstacles participants face in following these practices. What are some ways to overcome these obstacles?

# *Our Sales Philosophy*

To what extent do you agree or disagree with the following statements?

1. We ask customers to tell us what specific results would lead to their long-time satisfaction with our products or services.

   strongly disagree                            strongly agree
   1        2        3        4        5        6        7

2. We advise customers when their expectations seem unrealistic.

   strongly disagree                            strongly agree
   1        2        3        4        5        6        7

3. We are always honest and promise only what we can deliver.

   strongly disagree                            strongly agree
   1        2        3        4        5        6        7

4. We consult with our customers after the sale to learn how well their needs have been met.

   strongly disagree                            strongly agree
   1        2        3        4        5        6        7

5. We focus on the customers' needs and objectives even if it means that we must find new solutions to meet them.

   strongly disagree                            strongly agree
   1        2        3        4        5        6        7

6. We take the time to pull from customers what they need rather than push them to satisfy our needs.

   strongly disagree                            strongly agree
   1        2        3        4        5        6        7

7. We work hard at trying to put ourselves into our customers' shoes.

   strongly disagree                            strongly agree
   1        2        3        4        5        6        7

# 14 TEAM BUILDING

## 63 The Stages of Team Development: A Card Sorting Activity

### Introductory Remarks

Like babies, teams need to crawl before they can walk. The best-known terms to describe the stages of team development are *forming, storming, norming,* and *performing.* This activity is a fun way to understand these stages. It uses cards describing events that occur as teams develop. Participants must sort these events into the four stages. More than just being a fun sorting activity, it simulates how the mind sorts information to form concepts. It is also an effective activity for teaching teamwork.

## *Objectives*

- To understand inductively the four stages of team development.
- To work together, as a team, to complete a challenging task.

**Group Size:** any size.
**Time Required:** 30 minutes

## *Materials*

- A flip chart page on which you've written the terms Forming, Storming, Norming, and Performing
- A flat surface for each team, such as a table top

- One set of twenty index cards per team (see Step 3)

- One copy of the Is It Forming, Storming, Norming, or Performing? handout for each participant

## *Activity Flow*

1. Display the terms: forming, storming, norming, and performing. Ask who knows what they mean in terms of team development.

2. If many people know about what characterizes each stage, proceed with the card-sorting activity to be described. If few people know the terms (as opposed to "heard of them"), state the following:

"It takes time for teams to reach a point at which they are productive. Team members have a lot to work out with each other. At first, they are hesitant, waiting for direction from a 'leader.' Members are just getting their feet wet. The team is beginning the process of *forming*. As they get to know each other, some people are more outspoken and start to disagree with each other about some things. This period can be called *storming* because interaction becomes somewhat stormy. At some point, the team starts to work out some agreements or norms. Hence, the period is called *norming*. When those agreements have been reached, the team is in a better position to be collaborative and effective. They begin to act like a high-*performing* team.

"This progression doesn't always happen, however. A team may get stuck somewhere and not progress or, worse, may reverse direction. It takes a few months for teams to jell. Some teams never reach this point."

3. Form teams of three to six people. Give each team a set of twenty cards: four "header" cards that have one each of the four stages printed on them (forming, storming, norming, performing) and sixteen additional cards that contain the following statements (cards should include both the number and the statement):

   1. Members are concerned with acceptance.

   2. Leadership is shared.

   3. Team enjoys open, honest communication.

    4. Conflict continues to occur.

    5. Goals are not clear, but clarity is not sought.

    6. Team encourages innovation.

    7. Cohesion and trust increase.

    8. Members communicate in a tentative manner.

    9. Clarification of goals begins.

   10. Participation increases.

   11. Member satisfaction increases.

   12. Conflicts start to surface.

   13. The team leader is seen as benevolent and competent.

   14. Subgroups and coalitions form.

   15. Leader's role becomes more consultative.

   16. Subgroups work on important tasks.

4. Explain that their task is to work together to place the appropriate four statements about team development under each of the four header cards: forming, storming, norming, and performing.

5. After 10 or 15 minutes, stop the activity and distribute the Is It Forming, Storming, Norming, or Performing? handout. Provide the answers to the card sort as follows:

   - Forming: 1, 5, 8, 13
   - Storming: 9, 10, 12, 14
   - Norming: 4, 7, 11, 15
   - Performing: 2, 3, 6, 16

   Invite each participant to write down the "answers" at the bottom of the handout. Then have them count how many of their cards were correctly placed. Finally, have each team resort the cards correctly.

6. Explain the "answers" as follows:

   "Research on team development suggests that each of these sixteen events occur typically at a given stage. No event stops happening permanently, but is more likely to occur during a particular stage. When groups begin to form, members are somewhat anxious and concerned with acceptance by others (1). They are also tentative with each other (8) because they don't want to get off on the wrong foot. As a result, team goals are not debated or sharpened (5). A person who acts (officially or unofficially) as the team's primary leader usually is most welcomed, and the group depends a lot on this person (13).

"As members get more used to each other and less dependent on a primary leader, they start to debate the team's goals (9) and participation increases (10). That's the positive side of storming. However, conflicts start to surface in the debate (12) and team members may form two or more coalitions (14), much like what happens in a political climate, as opposed to a collaborative one.

"In the next stage, conflicts still occur (4) but, needing to move forward, important agreements are made. Cohesion and trust increase (7) and, as a result, member satisfaction increases (11). The leader's role changes from that of an expert to more of a consultant (15).

"As the team is more productive, leadership becomes more shared (2) and the team enjoys open, honest communication (3). The team encourages innovation (6) and trusts members to work in subgroups on important tasks (16)."

7. Obtain reactions to the "answers." Inquire whether they make sense. Add other comments you wish to make about the stages of team development.

# Other Options

1. Ask the entire group to dramatize a team at all of the four stages. Have the participants assume that a group is charged with making recommendations about creating a more "green" local community. Obtain volunteers from 25 percent of the entire group to start the first meeting of the group. Have them portray the events that might happen at this early forming stage. Next, recruit another 25 percent to portray the team at the storming stage. Continue with two more groups who will act out the norming and performing stages. Act as the overall director of the drama to provide direction and continuity.

2. With the group's help, create an analogy in which two people are developing a relationship. What would the forming, storming, norming, and performing stages in the relationship look like?

# Is It Forming, Storming, Norming, or Performing?

1. Members are concerned with acceptance.

2. Leadership is shared.

3. Team enjoys open, honest communication.

4. Conflict continues to occur.

5. Goals are not clear, but clarity is not sought.

6. Team encourages innovation.

7. Cohesion and trust increase.

8. Members communicate in a tentative manner.

9. Clarification of goals begins.

10. Participation increases.

11. Member satisfaction increases.

12. Conflicts start to surface.

13. The team leader is seen as benevolent and competent.

14. Subgroups and coalitions form.

15. Leader's role becomes more consultative.

16. Subgroups work on important tasks.

Forming: ___ ___ ___ ___

Storming: ___ ___ ___ ___

Norming: ___ ___ ___ ___

Performing: ___ ___ ___ ___

## **64** **Television Commercial: An Unusual Team-Building Activity**

### ─────**Introductory Remarks**─────

This is an excellent opening activity or icebreaker when group members work in a common field, organization, or unit. Or it can be converted into a challenging task that encourages lots of teamwork and creativity. The beauty of the activity is that you can make it as simple or elaborate as you would like. Participants are asked to create a TV commercial that advertises things of importance to their team, their profession, or organization. Doing this may take as little as 20 minutes or several hours. At a conference of physicians' assistants that I once facilitated, participants were placed into small teams and, with the help of video cameras (this occurred before cell phones), created entertaining commercials. The winning team received a small prize. The collective result was a source of pride to the participants and a moving tribute to their profession.

## *Objectives*

- To promote the work of a group or organization.
- To develop group cohesion and pride.

**Group Size:** teams of up to six members with no limit on the number of teams

**Time Required:** from 20 minutes to several hours

**Materials:** as you see fit

# *Activity Flow*

1. Divide participants into teams of no more than six members. Ask each team to share some qualities of their own team, department, profession, or organization.

2. Next, ask teams to create a 30-second television commercial that advertises their team, their profession, or their organization.

3. The commercial should contain a slogan (for example, "You are now free to move about the country") and visuals.

4. Explain that the general concept and an outline of the commercial are sufficient. But if team members want to act out their commercial, that is fine too.

5. Before each team begins planning its commercial, discuss the characteristics of currently well-known commercials to stimulate creativity (for example, the use of a well-known personality, humor, a comparison to the competition, or a slogan). Also, provide this example:

   "Employees of a hospital are asked to develop a television commercial that advertises the advantages of being a patient at their hospital. They create an advertisement that combines the slogans of several well-known commercials that emphasize care and friendliness, such as 'You're in good hands with Southwest Hospital' and 'When you care enough to provide the very best.'"

6. Ask each team to present its ideas. Praise everyone's creativity.

# **Other Options**

1. Have teams create print advertisements instead of television commercials or, if possible, have them actually create commercials on videotape.

2. Invite teams to advertise interests, values, beliefs, or concerns that shape their mission.

# 65 Creative House Building: An Exercise in Teamwork

---
## Introductory Remarks
---

In this activity, participants work in teams to construct a house with limited supplies. There is no competition in the exercise. With freedom to create whatever house they want, the results differ considerably among the teams. The experience is intensely personal to each team. You can use this activity as a team-building exercise or a creative problem-solving task.

## Objectives

- To demonstrate how creative people can be with limited resources.
- To build team cohesiveness.

**Group Size:** unlimited
**Time Required:** 30 minutes

## Materials

- Sets of index cards (of various sizes) for each team
- Assorted marking pens for each team

## Activity Flow

1. Divide participants into teams of four to six members and place them at their own tables. Provide each team with a stack of index cards (different sizes in each stack are best) and assorted marking pens.

2. Challenge each team to be the most creative group they can be by constructing a "house of their dreams" solely from the index cards. While folding, tearing, and drawing on the cards are permitted, no other supplies can be used for the construction.

3. Allow at least 15 minutes for the construction. Do not rush or pressure the groups. It is important for each to have a successful experience.

4. When the constructions are finished, invite the full group to take "a tour of the neighborhood." Visit each construction and request that team members show off their work and explain any intricacies of their house. Applaud each team's accomplishments.

5. Reconvene the teams and ask them to reflect on the experience by responding to these questions:

   - Were you surprised by what you and others could create with limited supplies?

   - What were some helpful and not so helpful actions you did as a group and individually when working together?

   - What have you learned that you can take back to your job?

# Other Options

1. Turn the activity into a team competition. State that the houses will be judged by three criteria:

   - Sturdiness

   - Height

   - Aesthetic appeal

   Award up to 10 points for each construction.

2. Have teams create a team totem pole instead of a house.

#  Fishbowl Meeting: Observing Group Process

---
**Introductory Remarks**
---

Asking the participants to take part in a fishbowl design is an excellent way to observe the dynamics or process of a group working on a problem or a task. In this activity, the participants get to observe another group work on a task, problem, or issue as they work on the same thing. Are the groups mirror images of each other or very different?

## *Objectives*

- To observe group process in a unique setting.
- To compare how two groups go about doing a similar task.

**Group Size:** up to twelve participants

**Time Required:** over 30 minutes

**Materials:** none

## *Activity Flow*

1. Set up a tight circle of chairs with a second circle directly outside the first. Both circles should have enough chairs to accommodate the number of participants you are expecting.

2. State the following:

   "Imagine that you are a part of a group that is charged with coming up with your top three ideas to improve the ways in which organizations relate to their employees."

3. Divide the entire group randomly into two subgroups. Explain that the two groups will have the same task. They will work on the task in two rounds. In each round, they will be observed by the other group.

4. Tell the first group to takes seats in the inner circle of chairs. Direct the second group to sit in the outer circle behind the others.

5. Ask those in the inner circle, Group A, to begin discussion. Direct those seated in the outer circle only to listen and observe and not to take part in the discussion. Allow 6 to 10 minutes for the discussion.

6. At the end of the time limit, ask the two groups to trade seats. Now Group B is in the inner circle and will have the same length of time to discuss recommendations while Group A members listen and observe. (Although the goal is for each group to come up with their own thoughts, they may borrow ideas and build on them during their time in the inner circle of the fishbowl.)

7. Have Groups A and B trade places again and each discuss additional ideas on how organizations might treat their employees better.

8. End the exchange and pair up participants, one from Group A and one from Group B. Ask the pairs to discuss the process of each group (not the content). Did each group go about the task in similar or contrasting ways? Did they have different styles of communication?

9. Reconvene the entire group and discuss the same questions.

# Other Options

1. Give each group different tasks and observe the resulting dynamics. In this option, you are probably better off having only one long round each.

2. Have only one group being observed. Give the observers some suggestions to look for before starting.

- How did leadership emerge in the group? What other roles emerged?

- Did the group develop an effective format or game plan for discussion and decision making?

- Was participation widespread?

- Did any conflicts emerge? If so, how were they handled?

# 67 Making Paper Cups: Simulating A Learning Organization

┌─────────────── **Introductory Remarks** ───────────────┐

In this simulation exercise, participants are asked to
follow directions to make a paper cup. Typically, some
participants are more adept at the task than others. Those
people become learning coaches whose task it is to make
sure that everyone is competent in making a paper cup
"with their eyes closed." I love this activity because it
shows how rapidly knowledge can be spread within an
"organization." The impact of the activity is stunning.

└────────────────────────────────────────────────────────┘

## Objectives

- To demonstrate the power of high expectations.
- To illuminate how quickly people can be effective coaches of others.
- To reinforce the power of learning organizations.

**Group Size:** unlimited.

**Time Required:** 20 to 30 minutes

## Materials

- One copy of the Instructions for Creating a Paper Cup handout for each participant
- A minimum of six square sheets of paper per participant (The best way to create squares is to use 8.5 × 11 paper and cut the 11-inch side down to 8.5 inches. Depending on the size of the group, use a paper cutter, if available, since eventually there needs to be a minimum of six cut

sheets per participant. An alternative is to photocopy an 8.5 × 11 sheet containing a horizontal dotted line at 8.5 inches of the 11-inch side. Ask participants to fold the paper on the dotted line and tear off the excess 2.5 inches.)

■ A sample completed cup

## *Activity Flow*

1. Distribute a square sheet of paper to each participant.

2. Distribute the Instructions handout to each participant. Explain that their "job" is to follow the directions to create a paper cup. Display a finished version so that everyone can see a completed cup. Inform them that, with the help of others, they will eventually be able to create a paper cup even "with their eyes closed." State that everyone must work on his or her own and cannot be helped by others.

3. Tell participants who have successfully created the cup to obtain an additional sheet located nearby. (If you have table groups, place several additional sheets on each table.) Challenge them to create another cup without referring to the instructions. Some participants are able to do this fairly quickly. Others are still struggling just following the instructions. This discrepancy in skill will create a lot of frustration, but encourage the "strugglers" to try again, using new sheets.

4. Request that those who have made a cup without looking at the instructions do so once again "with their eyes closed." If they are able to do so, they can do the task so well that they are now "certified cup makers." At this point, there are a few "certified" cup makers in the room. Ask them to coach others around them until those others also know the task so well they can perform it "with their eyes closed."

5. As time goes by, several "coaches" become available in the room. They can assist the ones who are still struggling, including verbal prompts and modeling. However, the participants must eventually be capable of making cups without direct help in order to move to the next level. The same requirement holds for participants making a cup with their eyes closed.

6. Expect that most, if not all, participants will be "certified" within 15 or 20 minutes. This result amazes the entire group.

7. Debrief the simulation by following the what, so what, now what sequence: What happened to you during this exercise? What were you feeling? Despite the challenging task (for many), what happened that allowed the seemingly impossible result to occur? What lessons can you take away from the simulations? What can you do to create this level of collaboration in your organization?

# Other Options

1. Convert this exercise to one that teaches about different styles of learning. Begin by giving the following verbal directions:

   - Fold the square in half along a diagonal to form a triangle. Hold the paper with the tip of the triangle facing up.
   - Fold the top point down to the bottom edge.
   - Unfold the square.
   - Fold the left point of the triangle to the middle of the opposite side.
   - Fold the right point of the triangle to the middle of the opposite side.
   - Fold down a single layer from the top.
   - Fold back the other single layer from the top.
   - The cup is now complete.

2. Now provide the Instructions handout for those who have not been successful and encourage the participants to continue trying to create the cup.

3. Offer to show step-by-step how to make the cup for those who still are not successful. Ask: "How do you explain that some people needed only verbal instructions, others needed a diagram, and still other needed a step-by-step demonstration? Can you relate this to anything that happens on the job?"

Point out that people learn in different ways and at different rates. Some are visual learners, others auditory learners, and still others kinesthetic learners, or they are varying combinations of all three. Explain that the frustration they experienced with this activity is similar to what their employees experience on the job.

4. Obtain an easy construction puzzle with enough pieces so that there is at least one piece per participant. Give out one or more pieces to each participant. Have them work together to complete the puzzle. Debrief how they collaborated and apply what they did to acting as a learning organization. Or give participants a challenging poem to interpret. Ask them to work together to understand the poem.

# *Instructions for Creating a Paper Cup*

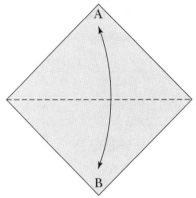

**1** Fold in half along a diagonal.

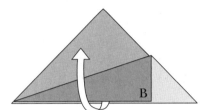

**3** ... like this. Unfold.

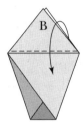

**6** Fold down single layer B

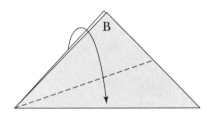

**2** Fold down corner B to
the bottom edge ...

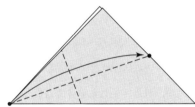

**4** Fold one dot to the other.

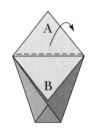

**7** Fold A behind.

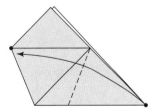

**5** Fold one dot to the other.

**8** The cup is complete

# 68 Are You a Team Player? Things Team Players Do

## Introductory Remarks

This short instrument gives respondents feedback on whether they are "team players" and in what specific areas they may want to improve. Use it whenever you are working with intact teams, especially when you want to focus on how each team member can contribute to the team's overall success.

## *Objectives*

- To assess participants as "team players."
- To discuss team areas of improvement.

**Group Size:** any size intact team

**Time Required:** 30 minutes

## *Materials*

- One copy of Are You a Team Player? assessment for each participant
- One copy of Interpreting Your Score for each participant

## *Activity Flow*

1. Distribute the Are You a Team Player? assessment. Ask participants to complete it.

2. Distribute the Interpreting Your Score handout. Ask participants to interpret their scores, using the handout as a guide.

3. Next, request that participants discuss the ten questions. Participants share their self-assessments and then react to others' self-assessments. (This can be done in pairs/small groups or as a whole team, depending on the size of your group.)

4. Finally, have the entire team discuss areas in which the team needs to improve.

# Other Options

1. Ask each team member to assess him- or herself without reference to the handout and share with the rest of the team what he or she is doing to be a team player. Invite other team members to give feedback.

2. Ask the team to visualize itself as an extremely effective team. Invite team members to share their thoughts with the goal in mind to answer three questions:

   - As a team, what should we STOP doing?

   - What should we START doing?

   - What should we CONTINUE doing?

# *Are You a Team Player?*

*Instructions:* As a member of a team, you can take a number of actions to contribute to the team's overall success. Rate how frequently you engage in the listed behaviors, using the following scale:

|  | Never | Occasionally | Often |
|---|---|---|---|
|  | 1 | 2 | 3 |

*Do you . . .*

| | Never | Occasionally | Often |
|---|---|---|---|
| 1. Pitch in and assist others? | 1 | 2 | 3 |
| 2. Interact with quiet or new teammates? | 1 | 2 | 3 |
| 3. Encourage teammates who are in conflict to talk out their differences? | 1 | 2 | 3 |
| 4. Share credit you get for a job well done? | 1 | 2 | 3 |
| 5. Suggest team-building/problem-solving techniques you may know? | 1 | 2 | 3 |
| 6. Check to see how your decisions might affect others? | 1 | 2 | 3 |
| 7. Include everyone in the information loop? | 1 | 2 | 3 |
| 8. Seek information and expertise of others? | 1 | 2 | 3 |
| 9. Communicate your own activity so that it is public knowledge? | 1 | 2 | 3 |
| 10. Inform others what they can do to support your efforts and ask them to tell you when they need help? | 1 | 2 | 3 |

When you have rated all ten items, add your responses to obtain your total score. Then use the Interpreting Your Score sheet to see how you rated yourself.

**Total:** _____

# *Interpreting Your Score*

Compare your total score to the following ranges:

26 to 30     You see yourself as having strong, effective collaborative behaviors and you use them consistently.

18 to 25     You believe you make some effort to collaborate with others, but see some room for improvement.

10 to 17     You know you're in trouble, but at least you're willing to admit it!

# 69 Paper Airplanes: The Power of Collaboration

## Introductory Remarks

In this exercise, participants are asked to make paper airplanes from sheets of paper. In the first attempts, nothing is done by the facilitator to encourage collaboration. Most likely, the majority of participants cannot create paper airplanes that fly. The experience is debriefed. Then the facilitator encourages the participants to collaborate. The results are dramatic. As a result, participants have a powerful experience in teamwork.

## *Objectives*

- To demonstrate how often people choose to work alone rather than collaborate with each other.
- To illuminate how quickly people give up when a task is beyond their skill level.
- To reinforce the power of collaboration.

**Group Size:** unlimited.

**Time Required:** 30 minutes

## *Materials*

- Five sheets of 8.5 by 11 paper per participant
- Masking tape
- A measuring tape
- A "target" (see Step 2)

# *Activity Flow*

1. Distribute five sheets of paper to each participant.

2. Tell the participants the following:

   "Let's see how many of you can make a paper airplane that flies effectively. You have 5 minutes. See whether your airplane can fly at least fifteen feet and hit a large target." (Suggest a target such as a flip chart or a presentation screen.)

3. Create a line made with the masking tape that participants cannot step over when thrusting their airplanes. The line should be approximately fifteen feet from the target.

4. Do not make any further comments. Adopt a noninvolved approach during the activity. Just observe what happens. Expect the following:

   - Most airplanes will nosedive or boomerang.

   - Most participants will make only one attempt.

   - Successful airplane makers will be cheered. However, few will show others how to be successful. Also, few will seek help. In addition, few, if any, participants will retrieve the effective designs to see how they were constructed. (Most participants will assume that such an inspection is tantamount to "cheating.")

5. After 5 minutes, stop the activity and debrief it, using the following questions as a guide.

   **What Happened?**
   - How did you feel (about your plane/effort)?
   - Did you try more than once? Why? Why not?
   - Did you look at others who had success? Why? Why not?
   - Did you ask for help? Offer help?

   **So What?**
   - What does this say about how we go about a task?
   - Deal with failure?
   - Work as a team?

6. Challenge the entire group to learn how to make a paper airplane that flies fifteen feet. Ask the group to suggest ways they can collaborate with one another. (For example, those with expertise can coach others or the characteristics of effective airplanes from the first round can be inspected and discussed.) Provide enough time for the vast majority to create and successfully fly their own paper airplanes.

7. Do a final debriefing. End with these questions:

**Now What?**

- How can we apply this experience to the work we do with others? (Specifically, how do we encourage ourselves to share our expertise and ask for help from others when we need it?)

- What else will we do differently in our efforts to work as a team?

# 15 TRAIN THE TRAINER ⸻

# 70 Active Vacations: Topics Versus Objectives

## Introductory Remarks

In this exercise, participants are asked to respond to a client's (Active Vacations, Inc.) request for a workshop intended for a first-time traveler's trip to Italy. The participants brainstorm topics for the workshop, only to realize that, without a sense of the objectives driving the workshop, it is impossible the select the content. This experience is usually a real eye-opener when training trainers.

## Objectives

- To experience how quickly a workshop design can be overwhelmed by many topical choices.

- To appreciate how the focus on outcomes is the first step in putting together a workshop or training session.

**Group Size:** any size

**Time Required:** 25 minutes

## Materials

- Flip chart or whiteboard and markers

## *Activity Flow*

1. Tell participants the following:

   "Active Vacations is a company that provides a travel package to visit three major destinations in Italy—Rome, Florence, and Venice. In the package, fees for air transportation, hotel accommodations, and transportation between the three cities are included. A half-day orientation sightseeing tour is also provided in each city. The remaining day and a half in each city is unstructured.

   "The company would like to provide a complimentary 90-minute workshop for people who have signed up for this package. It would be scheduled two weeks prior to departure at the headquarters of Active Vacations. We have been approached by Active Vacations to design the workshop. What topics should we cover?"

2. Invite input from participants until you receive ten to fifteen topics. Record the ideas so that all can see. Topics likely to emerge include:

   - major attractions
   - history of each city
   - shopping tips
   - currency conversion
   - basic Italian words and phrases
   - local customs
   - inner city transportation options
   - safety
   - medical and other emergencies
   - places to eat/types of restaurants

3. When you have reached ten to fifteen topics, stop the brainstorming process and ask participants to suggest how to prioritize the list, given the

fact that all these topics cannot be covered in 90 minutes! Expect differences of opinion to emerge. Keep the discussion going for at least 5 to 10 minutes OR until someone states, in so many words: "We can't prioritize the list until we decide what the major objective of the workshop is." If no participant states this, explain this point yourself. Then, elaborate with the following remarks:

"This exercise was set up to make the point that no training can be designed without coming to some decision about its goals or targets. The hallmark of good training is that it is based on objectives, not topics. When you decide what the objectives are, you can then decide on the content, but not before. In the case of Active Vacations, we would need to decide what we want the 90-minute workshop to achieve. Here are some possibilities:

- To allay the travelers' anxieties about the trip so that they approach it with confidence.

- To equip the travelers with knowledge and skills to maximize their unstructured time in each city.

- To motivate the participants to learn as much as possible about the major attractions prior to the trip."

Point out that the content and methods of a workshop would differ considerably from one of these objectives to another. Of course, the decision about objectives is not only ours. We should ask the client what they want to achieve as well. (Perhaps the client also has some useful assessment information to share.)

4. Reinforce this experience with these comments:

"It is not enough to simply list the topics you intend to cover. Training is constructed in terms of the achievement of objectives. The critical question, therefore, is not what topics to cover but what you want participants to value, understand, or do with those topics. A clear sense of where you want to go and what you are trying to accomplish is the single most important ingredient for designing effective training programs.

"Determining training objectives may take long-term thinking up-front, but it is worth it. Objectives are the pillars of your program, not straitjackets.

The single best reason to work hard on developing training objectives is that objectives drive your training design. When you are designing a training program, you are figuring out what steps will lead to the accomplishment of your objectives."

# Other Options

1. Provide a short list of training topics such as:

   - Teamwork

   - Leadership

   - Communication

   - Project management

   Have the entire group vote for one of these topics. Place participants in small groups and give each group 15 minutes to brainstorm what they might do in a 90-minute session on that topic. Have groups report their ideas. Observe the variety of ideas that are reported. Link this variety to the notion that each group, consciously or unconsciously, had varying objectives in mind when they made their decisions.

2. Discuss the importance of establishing objectives before beginning any project. Choose one or two projects as reference points. They can be work-related, such as planning a company picnic, or personal, such as designing a new kitchen.

**Design Challenges: Planning How to Achieve Training Objectives**

## Introductory Remarks

The most important consideration in designing any training activity is whether the activity achieves its purpose. The most creative activity in the world is of no value if it does not lead to an outcome a trainer is seeking. In this activity, you will challenge participants to create a design that achieves its stated objective. You will also challenge them to make effective decisions about such matters as *time allocation, key points and/or instructions, materials, setting,* and *ending.*

## *Objectives*

- To put together a brief training plan.
- To experience and practice conducting a short design.

**Group Size:** at least six participants
**Time Required:** 1 to 2 hours

## *Materials*

- One copy of the Designing Training Activities handout for each participant

## *Activity Flow*

1. Distribute the handout and give participants a few minutes to review it. Divide participants into pairs. Assign each pair one of the five objectives

so that each pair is working on a different objective. If you have more than ten participants, create one extra subgroup of any size and give them the role of participant-observers.

2.  Give pairs from 20 to 30 minutes to create their training designs. Have them select training plans to achieve their objectives, using methods such as case study, role play, visualization, and so forth. While they are preparing, have the participant-observers meet together and discuss how they might design some or all of the designs.

3.  Besides choosing a general plan, ask them to consider details such as *time allocation, key points and/or instructions, materials, setting,* and *ending.*

4.  Ask pairs to share their training plans with the entire group. Pairs can volunteer to present their plans whenever they feel ready to do so.

5.  Obtain feedback on each plan from other participants. The key question to be answered is whether the training plan achieves its objectives. Just staying on topic does not mean that the objectives will be achieved. For example, if the objectives involve learning a skill, does the design provide the participants a chance for the skill to be practiced? Discuss other design alternatives that will meet the standard of "fulfilling the objectives."

# Other Options

1.  If time permits, have the designers actually conduct all or parts of their training plans.

2.  Present a training plan for each objective that does NOT achieve its objective. Contrast that plan with one for which there is a match. For example, using the game *Charades* does not give participants feedback on their nonverbal behaviors beyond how they play *Charades.*

# *Designing Training Activities*

Following is a list of five training objectives. Put together a design lasting 20 minutes that achieves the objective to which you are assigned. Assume that the design occurs during the middle of a longer training sequence and that requisite knowledge for the design has already been accomplished. Limit your design to the objective specified.

Assume that there will be up to eight participants in the training.

1. Design a way for participants to obtain feedback from others about their nonverbal communication (for example, facial expression, body language).

2. Design a way to help participants get in touch with their feelings about confronting other adults (for example, problem employees).

3. Design a way to increase participants' knowledge of techniques for increasing the effectiveness of a meeting.

4. Design a way to enable participants to practice skills for facilitating discussions.

5. Design a way for participants to discuss their preferences about team ground rules.

# 72 Energizers: Ways to Wake Up or Relax a Training Group

## Introductory Remarks

There are many simple, short ways you can energize a new or tired training group or help a tense group calm down. You can do any of the energizers presented in this activity at the beginning of a training session, after a break, or right in the middle of the action. I find that when I choose one of these, it never fails to perk up a group and get them ready for experiential activities.

## *Objectives*

- To experience ways to energize a group.
- To connect an energizer to a topic.

**Group Size:** any

**Time Required:** 5 minutes

**Materials:** none

## *Activity Flow*

1. Choose one of the following to energize a group.

    - *Singing a round.* Section off participants and invite them to sing a familiar round such as "Row, Row, Row Your Boat."

    - *Slow breathing.* Invite participants to take ten slow, cleansing breaths—inhaling deeply and then exhaling. Then invite them to reverse the process. Have them start by slowly exhaling and then inhaling. Even though breathing is always a continuous cycle of inhaling and exhaling, consciously trying to emphasize each part of the cycle can be quite exhilarating.

- *Yawning contest.* See who can yawn the loudest or the longest.

- *Touch blue.* Call out a color (such as blue) and have participants scurry to touch any object of that color or person wearing it. Identify other things besides color, such as "something glass" or "something round." Or mention specific objects such as a watch, a book, sneakers, and so forth. Call the next item as soon as everyone has touched the current one.

- *Do the Hokey, Pokey.* You know . . . "Put your right (foot, arm, hip, etc.) in, put your right (foot, arm, hip, etc,) out, put your right (foot, arm, hip, etc.) in and shake it all about. Do the hokey, pokey, and turn yourself around. That's what it's all about."

- *Titles.* Give participants 1 minute to shout out the titles of as many films or books as they can. To make it more challenging, create more specifics, such as Hitchcock films, books by John Grisham, war films, management books, and so forth.

- *Back rubs.* Pair up participants and invite them to give each other back rubs. Or have participants line up in a circle, turning in the same direction. Have each of them give a back rub to the person in front of him or her. Then have them all turn in the opposite direction and give back rubs to the persons in front of them.

- *Human knot.* Ask participants to form a circle and clasp hands with two other people opposite them. Then ask them to unravel the tangle of hands and arms that has been created—without releasing their hands. The activity ends when the original circle is intact.

2. Transition to your topic. Make any connections you see between the energizer and what's to follow. For example, unraveling a human knot can be used as a segue to introduce the effective flow needed in managing a supply chain.

# Other Options ————————————————

1. Repeat the same energizer, instead of doing it only once. It can serve as an energy ritual for the group. Or alternate among several energizers.

2. Often, I invite a participant(s) to lead an energizer. (Give the participant(s) advance notice.) It's amazing how many are known in any group of people.

# 73 Has This Ever Happened to You? Making Team Learning Work

## Introductory Remarks

Placing participants in groups for learning purposes is fraught with problems. Because the trainer has far less control in this mode, so much depends on the skills and understanding of participants to work effectively without the constant leadership of the trainer. This activity gives participants an opportunity to strategize what to do so that the unfavorable things that occur can be minimized.

## *Objectives*

- To identify the variety of problems that team learning can bring.
- To brainstorm ideas to overcome these obstacles.

**Group Size:** any

**Time Required:** 30 minutes

## *Materials*

- One index card for each participant
- One copy of the Has This Ever Happened to You? handout for each participant
- Flip chart and markers

# *Activity Flow*

1. Explain that one of the most active forms of learning is when participants learn from one another. Unfortunately, this is easier said than done.

2. Distribute the Has This Ever Happened to You? handout.

3. Ask participants to check as many of the listed events as they have experienced when placing people in teams and giving them a small group learning activity.

4. You should find that your participants have experienced all or nearly all of the events. Explain that these represent the common obstacles to effective team learning and must be lessened in order to rely on team learning as an effective method. Obtain reactions.

5. Distribute one index card to each participant. Ask participants to each write one suggestion they would make to deal with any or all of these obstacles. Inform them that the cards will be anonymous. Urge them to write legibly since their cards will be read by others.

6. Collect the cards. Then randomly distribute one card to each participant. (It is okay if someone gets back his or her own card as long as he or she does not let anyone else know.)

7. Arrange people in trios and have them select the card with the best suggestion. Ask them to discard the two cards they don't want and place them in a spot accessible to every trio. Any trio can rummage through the discarded cards to find any card they prefer over the ones they already have read.

8. Invite each group to give a short report on the suggestion they have chosen. Record the suggestions on a flip chart.

9. Have the entire group reflect on the commonalties and diversity of suggestions among the subgroups.

10. Add any of your own suggestions. Here are some possibilities:

- Keep the team small.

- Make the task crystal clear.

- Obtain a team captain who will keep the team on task.

- Create other roles such as a timekeeper, recorder, or spokesperson.

- Have discussion rules, such as hearing from everyone once before someone can take a second turn.

- Make an agreement to share the load and do quality work.

## Other Options

1. Create teams of four to six participants. Simulate the problems listed in the handout by (secretly) giving cards to some participants directing them to engage in unhelpful behaviors. Observe how others respond.

2. Place participants into learning teams. Give them a well-known "survival" exercise such as *Lost on the Moon, Arctic Expedition,* or *Desert Survival.* As time goes by, some of the problems of working in teams should emerge. Interrupt the teams' work and make some suggestions to improve their team process. At the completion of the exercise, debrief the effectiveness of the interventions.

# *Has This Ever Happened to You?*

Check which events you have experienced when participants are placed in groups and given learning assignments.

☐ *Confusion:* They don't know what to do because they didn't follow the directions.

☐ *Tangents:* They don't stick to the topic or, worse yet, they talk about something else.

☐ *Unequal participation:* Some people dominate, some remain quiet.

☐ *One-way communication:* They don't listen and respond to each other.

☐ *No division of labor:* Some people don't pull their own weight.

☐ *Superficiality:* They're done before you know it, breezing through the task in the fastest way possible.

# 74 Training Styles: Three Continua

---

## Introductory Remarks

Here is a fun way to get participants to assess their "training styles." It uses a technique in which participants place themselves physically among other participants to indicate some critical choices each makes as a trainer. The activity works well on its own or combined with other activities.

---

## *Objectives*

- To introduce the concept of "training style."

- To consider changes participants may want to make in their styles.

**Group Size:** up to sixteen participants

**Time Required:** 20 minutes

**Materials:** none

## *Activity Flow*

1. Participants should be seated in a circle. Explain that you will be using a technique called "physical continua." Each time you state a continuum, participants should rearrange clockwise according to the continua (or spectrum).

2. To get participants to practice forming continua, try these two:

   Rearrange yourselves by height .

   Rearrange yourselves by birthdays.

3. Tell them that you want to do the same with "training style." You will provide two ends of three continua. Deciding where they belong in the circle will be less clear than in the practice step. To achieve a rearrangement each time, the participants will have to discuss their approaches or training styles with each other.

4. Ask participants to arrange themselves according to how they see their style as *instructor-centered* or *participant-centered*. The former maintains the instructor as the central focus person during training sessions. The latter seeks to encourage peer learning and even peer teaching.

5. Next, ask participants to share why they placed themselves as they did. Allow participants to trade placements as more information is shared.

6. Then ask participants to share whether they are happy with their current styles or not.

7. Continue the same process for two more continua: *well-planned* versus *spontaneous* (Are you meticulous in your planning? How much do you allow for spontaneity?) and *instructive* versus *experiential* (How many of the key points come from you? How much do you allow participants to learn from their own experience?).

   Be careful to point out that the end points of each continua are equally valid. One end is not better than the other.

8. Ask participants what they conclude about their training style from their placement on all three continua. Are they happy with their current styles or do they want to make changes?

# Other Options

1. Have participants complete the Trainer Style Inventory by Jean Barbazette. (See Chapter 2 in *The Art of Great Training Delivery*, Pfeiffer, 2006.) Barbazette's styles are *Instructor, Explorer, Thinker,* and *Guide.*

2. Have participants complete the Instructional Styles Diagnosis Inventory by Karen Lawson. (See Chapter 3 in *The Trainer's Handbook*, Pfeiffer, 1998.) Lawson's styles are *Seller, Coach, Professor,* and *Entertainer.*

## 75 You Have Many Options: Increasing Your Training Repertoire

───────── **Introductory Remarks** ─────────

One of the reasons I like being a trainer is that there are
almost always choices I have in designing and facilitating. I
can be creative and match the needs of a specific situation.
When training others to train, I like to invite them to tap
into the many options. In this activity, participants are asked
to brainstorm different ways to accomplish their goals. It
stretches their repertoire and unleashes lots of ideas.

## Objectives

- To show that there are several options for conducting training.
- To increase participants' ability to use different options.

**Group Size:** any

**Time Required:** 30 minutes

## Materials

- Newsprint and markers for each group

## Activity Flow

1. Divide participants into groups of three or four.

2. Explain that every trainer has options to conduct his or her own training. Different options may have advantages and disadvantages, but the best option at any moment may not be the one commonly chosen.

3. Give each group newsprint and a marker and assign one of the following topics to each group, choosing those of greatest benefit to the trainers you are training:

   - The physical organization of the training room (especially tables and chairs)

   - Formats for role playing

   - Making your training presentations more visual

   - Alternatives to lecturing

   - Things participants can do in pairs

   - Strategies for forming groups

   - Times to use case studies

   - Blended learning solutions

   - Needs assessment methods

   - Ways to increase participation

4. For their assigned topic, each group is to brainstorm different ways of accomplishing the topic.

5. Ask groups to present the option lists they have created. Invite questions and comments from fellow participants. Add a few options of your own.

# Other Options

1. Invite participants to explore The Nuts and Bolts of Active Training in *101 Ways to Make Training Active* (2nd ed.) by Mel Silberman (Pfeiffer, 2005). It contains two hundred training options.

2. Convert the activity into a competitive game. One way to do this is to organize your group into teams. Call out the categories on the list from above one-by-one. The team that comes up with the most options for each category wins.

# ABOUT THE AUTHOR

**Mel Silberman** was described as "the Leonardo Da Vinci of experiential learning—a scholar, inventor, engineer, and artist." For more than thirty-five years, he created and facilitated experiential activities in a wide variety of topics.

Mel was a psychologist known internationally as a pioneer in the areas of active learning, interpersonal intelligence, and team development. As professor of adult and organizational development at Temple University, Mel won two awards for his distinguished teaching. He was president of Active Training, in Princeton, New Jersey, a provider of products, seminars, and publications in his areas of expertise. He had more than thirty-five years of experience creating and honing techniques that inspire people to be people smart, learn faster, and collaborate effectively.

Mel shared his original and practical ideas throughout his books and through active training programs and customized seminars for corporate, educational, human services, and governmental organizations. His training skills, psychological insights, and engaging personality made him a popular speaker at conferences of the American Society for Training and Development, the International Society for Performance Improvement, *Training* magazine, Professional and Organizational Network in Higher Education, and the North American Simulation and Gaming Association.

A graduate of Brandeis University, Mel received his Ph.D. in educational psychology from the University of Chicago. He was also a licensed psychologist in the State of New Jersey.

His book, *101 Ways to Make Training Active*, was voted one of the five best training and development books of all time by *Training* magazine. Among his other publications are

- *Active Training: A Handbook of Techniques, Designs, Case Examples, and Tips* (3rd ed.)

- *Active Learning: 101 Strategies to Teach Any Subject*

- *101 Ways to Make Meetings Active*

- *PeopleSmart: Developing Your Interpersonal Intelligence*

- *Teaching Actively*

- *The Consultant's Toolkit*

- *The Consultant's Big Book of Reproducible Surveys and Questionnaires*

- *The Consultant's Big Book of Organization Development Tools*

- *The Active Manager's Toolkit*

- *The Best of Active Training, Volumes I and II*

- *Training the Active Training Way*

- *The 60-Minute Active Training Series*

- *Working PeopleSmart: Six Strategies for Success*

Mel served as editor of *The ASTD Training and Performance Sourcebook* and *The ASTD OD and Leadership Sourcebook*. He was also editor of the recently published book, *The Handbook of Experiential Learning*.

Recently, Mel was honored with a Lifetime Achievement Award at the annual conference of the North American Simulation and Gaming Association.